The

OUTCOMEMODEL™
The Time-Tested System for Achieving Goals

By Bruce Morrow

Designed By Ken Szpindor

ISBN 978-1-61623-922-0

This book is dedicated to Mark "Craze" Stewart, a great friend, a larger-than-life human being, a wonderful father and husband, a "Georgia Bulldog," and a character whose absence makes all our lives a little lonelier.

CONTENTS

ACKNOWLEDGEMENTS

When I set out to write this book, I had no idea what a group exercise it would become. I want to thank every single person who helped me talk through the idea, put it down on paper, fix it, and get it ready for publication.

First, the people who were involved in developing the Outcome Model™ for our business, M²Creative: Amy Reed, who is our poster child for caring more about clients' outcomes than anybody else in the world and who practiced it long before we put a name to it; Pete Foley, who is a tremendous sounding board and gifted communicator; Barb Mock, whose focus on putting thoughts into action in our business provides perspective on how this way of thinking affects the overall operation; Derek Fugaro, whose offbeat humor provides the perfect environment for creative thinking and human resources intervention; Amanda Jomaa, who is the only evidence I have that sane people can thrive in this business; Janene Jackson who has proven that the Outcome Model™ can be put to use in finance as well as communications, Betty Felton, whose enthusiasm for selling with the Outcome Model™ is an inspiration to me and to her colleagues; and my business partner Mike Yag for embracing the concept and applying it to his business as well. Thanks for the free focus group.

A very special thank you goes to Ken Szpindor, the ultra-talented graphic designer and creative mind, who not only makes it a pleasure to come to work every day, but whose tireless work on the design and execution of this book has made it look at least 50% better than it is.

Thanks to Linda Kush, my sister, the Harvard graduate and meticulous editor, who not only puts up with my brother on a regular basis, but whose willingness to tackle this project with her professional eye was the greatest compliment to me. Thanks to Spencer Morrow, my brother, who despite hating anything even approaching a "business book" offered his encouragement and compliments and kept Wil-BUH from eating the manuscript.

And finally, special thanks to Ed Hoard, my golf pro inspiration from Chapter 1, who taught me that even bad golfers can score well occasionally. Ed passed away unexpectedly at the age of 63 while I was writing the book, and we miss him, that Gator in a Bulldog town.

FIRST PLACE

INTRODUCTION

How Thoughts Become Things

I Live In a Van

Down By The River

"One man's magic is another man's engineering."

- Goethe

My friend Pete Foley believes thoughts become things. I agree. I've seen the result of this kind of thinking. I've seen friends who are sick or hurt heal faster and better than anyone thought they could. I've seen businesspeople with clear ideas turn them into thriving companies. I've seen social workers with vision change the very nature of communities. Thoughts do become things.

Great athletes employ mental imaging. They envision the result before they face the test. It could be a free throw or a five-iron. The player sees the ball going into the hoop or onto the green in his mind's eye, and then he executes.

Before they go on stage, politicians and performers form a mental picture of what they want the audience to do. How their appearance turns out often depends upon what they see when they close their eyes and invent that image.

This notion of thoughts becoming things seems like magic. The successful application of mental imaging is almost otherworldly when it results in something marvelous like a record-breaking mile or a perfect 10 on the balance beam.

But it isn't magic. It's not even unusual. In fact, a thought becoming a thing is the most natural and ordinary and repeatable action in the world. It's no more magical than dirt turning into mud. You take dirt. You add water. You make mud.

A desired outcome becomes reality when we make it so. In fact, achieving an outcome without envisioning it, studying it, or determining what

3

changes will be necessary to getting there… isn't an achievement at all. It's an accident.

Thoughts do become things. But don't let the extraordinary nature of the phenomenon obscure the really important middle ground between the thought and the thing. That's where the work gets done. And it's the key to The Outcome Model™.

The Outcome Model™ requires a vision; a destination; a clear and expressed understanding of what you choose your outcome to be; a clear image of your result; a willingness to give in to the audacious belief that once you identify it, it will be so.

But don't mistake this book for a pep talk, and don't mistake me for a motivational speaker. I don't live in a van down by the river, and I'm not remotely interested in making anybody feel good. Living The Outcome Model™ is a discipline that requires commitment to hard work, intellectual vigor, open-minded acceptance of possibly uncomfortable truths, recognition of weaknesses as well as strengths, and dogged determination.

Outcome thinking may be counter-intuitive. It might burst bubbles or put cracks in the patina of accepted practice. It might show somebody that he or she is wrong.

Living The Outcome Model™ requires an absolute commitment to the outcome. Because, if you do it right, the outcome is exactly what you're going to get.

Oh, and lest I fail to mention this several dozen times between now and beer-thirty, outcome thinking hates buzz words, cursory examinations, foregone conclusions, know-it-all leadership, distracted participation, spin, digression, grandstanding, and armchair quarterbacking (among other things). It is a participatory discipline, just like practicing the piano, lifting weights, perfecting the swimming stroke, or learning organic chemistry. You can't do it with a Blackberry® in your hand.

I'm a very good pitch guy. And for years, I've tried to figure out why. I'm actually kind of shy. I'm not a We Are the World kind of "People-Person." I don't naturally take to the task of convincing anybody of anything, and I'm certainly not the Chairman of the Personality Department here at the University of Group Dynamics.

But after about 30 years at it, I've finally been able to trace my success to this single approach: I am an outcome communicator. My success isn't an accident or a freak of nature... or even the just desserts of a good life well lived. I practice the discipline of the Outcome Model™ in everything I do that works. When I don't practice it, my success rate plummets.

Outcome thinking makes winning fun, because you earned it. As a particularly astute former football coach lamented to our remarkably mediocre team back in the early seventies: "Boys, winning don't just happen! What the hell fun would that be?"

What fun, indeed?

CHAPTER ONE

A Way of Thinking

"Have you ever noticed what golf spells backwards?"

- Al Boliska

A friend of mine really changed my perspective on business and achievement. I haven't paid him for it yet, and I probably never will, but maybe I'll put his picture in this book. I'm sure he'd be happy to hear that I'm sharing it with you. Just don't tell him you paid for it.

The funny thing is, he's not a traditional business guy. He's a golf pro. Ed Hoard played his collegiate golf at the University of Florida and has spent his career as a club and teaching professional. He became the Chairman of the PGA Rules Committee, and you've probably seen him on television officiating some of the major tournaments.

He's the one in the hat.

Anyway, while he knows what he's talking about when it comes to golf, I never imagined what he could do for my business. But after one day with him, I gained a new and powerful understanding of what works and doesn't work in my business and in my thinking. You'll be amazed at how simple and effective it is.

In the interest of full disclosure, it's important to understand that I normally play with a bunch of reprobates whose approach to the tee shot can be summed up in two words: "Kill It." We play in what I call the Brett Favre style. Get it out there as far as you can no matter how much trouble you see. If something goes wrong, either duck or get the hell out of the way.

It's an interesting group:

- Craze, the former University of Georgia football captain who turned to insurance after a "humorous" stint in the Secret Service;

- Johnny, a financial planner who has a pathological hatred for that insurance gecko on TV;

- Walter, the venture capitalist who's so cheap he brings his own peanut butter and banana sandwich and Coke to the course with him, rather than buy a two-dollar hot dog; and

- Me, a corporate communications guy who's got plenty of quirks of his own which he's not about to share here.

Between us we've got a bad knee, a bad back, recent heart surgery, and a cabin in Montana, so usually one of us is missing. We tried to fill in with one guy, but he talks too much and way too authoritatively, which irritates Walter in a deep, seething, loose-screw kind of way.

Not long ago, our fourth was Ed Hoard.

As Club Pro, Ed will often stand around the first tee and makes comments under his breath or, worse, try to teach me something. It usually starts with a sentence like, "Bruce, before you tee off, I want you to think about just one thing…" This is guaranteed to screw me up for at least six holes while I try to get it out of my head. It's sort of like somebody whistling "Knock Three Times on the Ceiling if You Want Me" on the subway. How are you supposed to go on with your day after that?

Fortunately, Ed had decided to join us rather than teach us, and when golf balls were tossed, he was my partner. And it's in his golf game that I found the secret to business and communications. And, we won the

Nassau.

Ed thinks backwards.
This is not a slight on the University of Florida. It's true. Ed thinks backwards. And I began to notice this right off the bat when we played together.

The first hole of the Donald Ross track we play on is very straightforward. About 430 yards down a hill, over a creek, and up a hill to a green that slopes steeply toward the front left. Some of the flat-bellies who belong to our club can drive the creek, but we can't, so it's pretty much all systems go from the tee.

Or so I thought.

In our group, one player's strategic discussion with his partner might go something like this:

> PLAYER ONE: You want me to go first?
> PLAYER TWO: Rip it.

But this time, while Johnny was "ripping it" over the cart path and into the sixth fairway, Ed was whispering questions to me. First, he asked me about the green.

> ED: See where the flag is today? What's that tell you?

The flag was on the upper right side of the green, about three paces off the edge, and guarded by a shallow bunker.

> BRUCE: What do you mean?
> ED: How are you going to make that putt?
> BRUCE: What putt?
> ED: What kind of putt do you want?
> BRUCE: Um, I don't know… short, straight and uphill?

ED: Exactly.

Then he asked me how I was going to approach the hole. I knew this was a trick question, because why would a pro ask a rank amateur with a rising handicap and a bad back how he was going to play the hole?

BRUCE: Um, okay. I'll hit a driver down the hill and a three-iron up to the green and then one putt for a birdie.
ED: I doubt it.

I guess what he was trying to say was this: given my handicap, a par was a perfectly reasonable outcome (since I would take the hole with a net birdie). We should see an actual birdie as a wonderful, albeit unlikely, surprise, something like the appearance of a rare emerald hummingbird at Lambeau Field on a football Sunday… late in the year.

He had a point. I was designing my approach around my fantasy and his game. Unfortunately, I don't have his game, and most of my fantasies by their very nature don't reflect much in the way of reality. So he told me to identify a realistic outcome and start thinking backwards.

What he meant by this was simple. In order to approach a golf hole, you have to think from the hole backwards, not the other way around. In a results-oriented profession, whether it's golf or business, you've got to start with the result—the outcome—and work your way back from there. It's only when you think backwards, from the outcome… that you can make all the right decisions along the way.

Okay, so if I wanted a short, straight, uphill putt, there was actually only one place I could put the ball on this particular green with the hole where it was. If I was above the hole, I was dead. If I was in the bunker, I was dead. If I was on the far right side of the green, I was, well, in a word, dead.

In fact, the last time I had played this hole, I hit a driver down the hill, a bladed three-iron worm-burner up to the green (above the hole by 30 feet), putted off the green, chipped above the hole again, lipped out on a racer downhill, and made a long putt coming back for a double bogey. It's like that old joke where the guy says "how in the world did you make a nine on that hole?" and the other guy answers, "I sunk a long putt!"

It's no way to spend a Saturday afternoon. And it's certainly no way to spend a career.

We started with the Outcome.
So we started with a realistic goal. A par was achievable as a reasonable outcome for my game. Facts, trends and history told us that it was un-likely I would make the par with a typical "greens-in-regulation" methodology, since my greens-in-regulation average was well below one-in-ten for this hole. And finally, it was easily measurable, because we were counting strokes.

THE OUTCOME MODEL™ ETERNAL TRUTH
A desired outcome must be relevant, realistic, and measurable.

We both knew exactly where we wanted the ball to be for an easy, up-hill putt. The question was how we were going to get it there. So we started talking backwards to get to the answer.

What was the best, most realistic place to be shooting from to get that short uphill putt? Realistically? It would be my third shot, a chip, from the left side. I was a pretty good chipper, and if I was short of the green on the left, I'd be chipping uphill and reasonably straight. It was a shot I was comfortable executing. Not pretty, but so what? As they all say, in golf, "it's not how; it's how many." We settled on a seven-iron chip from short left.

Wow. That gave me all kinds of new options for my second shot, none of which included heavenly intercession. We'd just opened up the landing area for shot number two by a ton. Before, when I was slashing away with a low iron, I was coming home on a swing and a prayer. Now I could think about another club and a wider landing area. Maybe I could use a five-iron (which is where I start getting comfortable with irons again), or even a six.

All I had to change was my behavior.
I have all of these shots in my bag! Not only that, but I was simplifying the game and taking all kinds of voodoo things out of my head. You know, it's the voodoo things running around in your head that account for lots of bad decisions and bad shots.

Voodoo things in business generally present themselves as nagging fears, unsupported concepts, ego-driven decision making, and stuff like that. Voodoo things in golf usually have to do with grip, pace, head movement, club selection, the last shot in the woods, and so forth. Voodoo things in your head are bad, and The Outcome Model™ helps eliminate them if you are willing to change your behaviors to achieve your desired outcome.

THE OUTCOME MODEL™ ETERNAL TRUTH
Outcome thinking requires specific changes in behavior related to achieving the desired outcome.

Let's review. Ed has me thinking backwards from the desired outcome.

Outcome: In the hole for a par
Shot #4: A short, straight, uphill putt (makeable!)
Shot #3: An uphill chip from the left side of the green (a rare strength!)
Shot #2: A manageable iron to a *wide* landing area (doable!)

All that's left is the drive. If you travel back in time to the description of my foursome and our enthusiastic (and manly) embrace of the "grip it and rip it" methodology, you'll recall that we're all about "going long" even if it means:

BRUCE:	Damn, I really crushed that one!
CRAZE:	Yeah, that ball went clear over the train tracks!

In the outcome scenario, however, the length of the drive is less important than where it lands. When I "crush" a driver, I usually lose it "a little" to the left. That means my second shot has to be toward the center-right or right of the green (or in a proximal bunker that they've stamped my name into just like they do to the sand in ashtrays at fancy hotels... I've been there that much), because I'm blocked by trees on the left.

By thinking first about the outcome, I've discovered that I need to be on the left side of the green, which means I want my drive to be toward the right side of the fairway. I could take a shorter club and get a better result! Whoa.

So the drive becomes a different animal than it had been. It becomes a domesticated animal, rather than a feral, infected she-cat with rabies, rat guts in her teeth, and a bad attitude.

It becomes a simple three-wood to the right side of the valley.

I made a par, a net birdie, and I won the hole for our team. I know; it's just like a fairy tale. Of course, on the second hole I took three shots to get out of a greenside bunker, and Craze declared that playing with me was better than going to Disney World, and he "didn't even have to buy a ticket."

But that's not the point. I'd learned a very valuable lesson that was easily applicable to my business. And when I started applying it, amazing things started happening.

I promised this wasn't a book about golf.

15

And I meant it. It's just that Ed Hoard had taken everything I ever thought about goal attainment and broken it down into manageable pieces that made sense in my world. There was actually a *method to the madness!*

And that's my last golf story, unless I think of another one.

So, with my fascinating adventure as our foundation, here's the official definition of The Outcome Model™.

> *The Outcome Model™ is the application of a logical series of actions which are informed and driven by a desired outcome and result in the achievement of that outcome. The success of the process is measured only by the achievement of the outcome.*

Oh, sure, all you MBA guys are snickering that it took me fifty-something years to figure this out. But those of us out there selling our stuff and actually producing the products (instead of sitting in the office looking at pie charts and using words like "granular" and "synergy") need a *methodical, repeatable, and effective* way to get out there and understand our customers and produce to their outcomes. So let's leave the bitterness and pedantry aside and talk about becoming hugely successful in whatever field we practice.

The Outcome Model™ is the way to do that. It can be applied to sales. It can be applied to product development. It can be applied to service. It can be applied to marketing. It can be applied to corporate communications. It can be applied to dating. Or asking your brother-in-law for a loan.

This book is a godsend.
I don't mean to sound immodest, but it's true. This book will teach you how to use The Outcome Model™. It will give examples of how it works best. It will give you ways to apply it to your own business. It will help you sell better, manage better, communicate better and learn more. And

it will help you become an Outcome thinker all the time.

As a true outcome thinker, you will be head-and-shoulders above your competitors. You will be a valuable advocate for your customers. You'll be able to enhance people's lives and businesses. And guess what? They'll gladly pay you for it.

As Craze says as he looks over a thirty-five-foot double breaker: "Bank it."

CHAPTER TWO
The Outcome Model™

"Our belief at the beginning of any doubtful undertaking is the one thing that assures the successful outcome of any venture. "

- William James

There's nothing magical about The Outcome Model™, other than the fact that it seems to do miracles for your business. It's really more of a discipline than a prescription, and its success depends upon your ability to ask hard questions and dig more deeply than is typical in today's "Blackberry Business" environment.

You can't do outcome thinking while text messaging.

So give your thumbs a rest and concentrate on what made all the great business leaders great. After all, some form or another of outcome thinking is what created the better mousetrap, the Model T, the moon landing, Marriott and Microsoft. It's got a pretty good track record.

You have to care about the outcome.
Here's a quick story about how we came to engage in Outcome Thinking and ultimately design The Outcome Model™.
In his bestseller *Good to Great*, Jim Collins describes the "Hedgehog Con-

cept" as the intersection of the following three things:

1. What you can be the best in the world at;
2. What drives your economic engine; and
3. What you are deeply passionate about.[1]

You have to understand: I absolutely hate most business books, and I have a deep-seated belief that the vast majority are written by people who couldn't make it in business if their daddy was Donald Trump. But this Jim Collins guy knows his stuff, precisely, I think, because he backed his conclusions out of reality rather than the other way around. He didn't make stuff up; rather, he gleaned stuff from reality, and it's amazing how well that works! The Outcome Model™ works the same way.

Jim Collins' "Hedgehog Concept" made great sense to us when we applied it to our business. We began by putting everybody in our office to the task of figuring out what our "Hedgehog Concept" was. And the group came up with this:

> *"We care more than anybody else in the world about our clients' outcomes."*

We may not be the biggest company doing what we do; we may not be the best capitalized; we may not have the most technology or the largest staff. But we can—*by our choice and through our passionate pursuit*—care more than anybody else in the world about our clients' outcomes. We have that choice in how we act, who we hire, and how our business is run day to day. We can make that choice. We can be the best in the world at that.

We should! It makes financial sense. We know from our history that our most profitable and sustainable clients have always been the ones for whose outcomes we cared the most. And caring came first. We were deeply invested in their outcomes—for whatever reason—before they

---

[1] Jim Collins, *Good to Great* (New York, N.Y.: HarperCollins Publishers, 2001), 90-96.

became intensely loyal or consistently profitable. You can see the trend. These clients clearly drive our economic engine. And we're passionate about them.

We found our "Hedgehog Concept" right around the same time I discovered that best results start with the outcome and work backwards. So now, not only did we care more about our clients' outcomes than anybody else in the world. We could actually do something about it!

So, we took everything we'd learned about golf (not much), combined it with everything we believed about taking care of our customers (a lot), and tried to make sense out of the process.

We knew we always achieved our clients' desired outcomes when we focused heavily on them and invested in them intellectually, creatively, and emotionally. We just had to take what we must have been doing intuitively and put it into a process that would create a discipline for the way we think and the way we act.

Don't mistake discipline for a lack of passion or creativity.
Outcome thinking does not remove creativity or passion from the process. It actually focuses them and enhances their effectiveness. If you took the model I'm going to show you and removed creativity, passion, and experience from the process, it would be like a Jungle Jim without any kids swinging on it. Sad and useless.

THE OUTCOME MODEL™ ETERNAL TRUTH
Outcome thinking requires passion, creativity, experience, and knowledge, all focused in a disciplined way.

Here's what the model looks like:

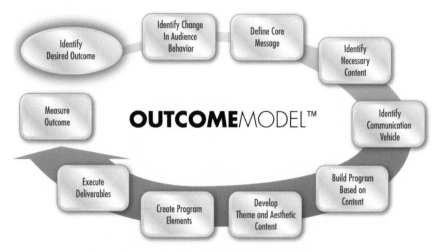

Outcome thinking begins with identifying the desired outcome, working your way through each subsequent step, and then measuring whether or not you achieved it. That's the "thoughts become things" part. You think it, you work it, and you achieve it.

However, the achievement of the desired outcome is not only dependent on your choice or your "mental imaging" of the outcome itself. It is absolutely dependent on the choices you make as you back your way through the process.

THE OUTCOME MODEL™ ETERNAL TRUTH
The achievement of a desired outcome will depend on the path you take and the choices you make.

That's why there are ten little boxes instead of just two.

The Outcome Model™ is both a process and a discipline. You have to cover all the bases in order to be an outcome thinker. That's the discipline part. You can't be an outcome thinker if you only commit to the first three or four steps. That would result in thinkus-interruptus, in which you talk a good game without ever committing to or being accountable for the desired outcome.

You've probably known people who engage in thinkus-interruptus. You may have even dated them. But, if you're like me, you'd never marry one.

THE OUTCOME MODEL™ ETERNAL TRUTH
The Outcome Model™ requires those who use it to commit to all the steps and accept accountability for the outcome.

That's because the overall purpose of living The Outcome Model™ is to achieve the outcome, not just talk about it! Some people in business don't really get this. I've got an old friend who is adamant about the difference between activity and productivity. If you're not willing to see the process through to the successful achievement of the outcome itself, it is a waste of your time to engage in the exercise to begin with.

Imagine being surrounded by people who only talk about stuff and never *do* anything. That would be hellish. That would be like spending eternity in a Cable Network Newsroom, where all the "breaking news" is really just old news. I don't know about you, but old news doesn't pay the bills in my business.

And don't start talking all "corporate."
You're not engaging in outcome thinking to impress anybody (although you will); you're not doing it to flap your gums; you're not doing it to "reach out to others in the enterprise in order to create a foundation for synergies." This is "Corporate Speak", and I'll say the same thing about it that Calvin Coolidge said when they asked him what he though about sin: "I'm against it."

The Steps
The Outcome Model™ is a lot like old-fashioned Christmas tree lights when you were a kid. Wired in series, if you fail to complete one of the steps correctly (as in one bulb goes out), the rest gets screwed up, too (as in all bulbs go out). Learn well. It's a tangled mess if you don't. Here's a quick overview of the steps.

Identify the Desired Outcome.

The identification of the desired outcome is a lesson in separating the wheat from the chaff. If you're not a wheat farmer you may not know what "chaff" is; it's the inedible stalks and stems and husks. Your Outcome, like whole wheat, has to be digestible. It also has to be relevant, realistic, and measurable. Not as easy as you think.

Identify the Changes in Behavior Required.

This step is all about identifying the changes in peoples' behavior that will be necessary to achieve the desired outcome. Identifying those necessary changes and actions is the first step to making them.

Develop the Core Message.

The core message defines the cause and effect relationship between changed behavior and the desired outcome. It is a clear statement that a specific action will result in the achievement of a specified outcome. A great example from popular film: "If you build it, he will come."[2]

Identify the Necessary Content.

This is the information you need to deliver to your audience, so they have the tools to make the change you're asking for. Content is the what, why, when, where, and how of The Outcome Model™.

Choose a Communication Vehicle.

This step is about choosing how to deliver the critical content in a way that is compelling, motivating, and effective. Choosing a communication vehicle should be an objective exercise. Whether you produce a meeting, a video, a commercial spot, a training module, or a sales presentation, you should do it because it's the best vehicle to drive the outcome.

Build the Program.

This is the stage where you actually begin to visualize the elements

---

[2] *Field of Dreams*, Universal Studios, 1989.

of the program itself. You create a virtual "storyboard" of what the program might look like, based on the desired outcome, the core message, and the necessary content. If it's a meeting, this might be a draft of the agenda. If it's a video, it may very well be a storyboard. If it's a sales pitch, it might be a slide deck or a written proposal.

Develop the Theme and Aesthetic Content.

The theme and aesthetic content are the language of your delivery. They create a familiar context for your target audience. A lot of people think they should begin with a broad theme and then "drill down" (Corporate Speak warning) to content and outcome. They would be wrong. The theme is derived from the desired outcome, period. It is anything but "broad." It may be all-encompassing, but that suggests depth rather than breadth.

Create the Program Elements.

This is the stuff you need to support your program. If it's a meeting, it might be audio-visual and staging. If it's a campaign, it might be graphic development or commercial spots. If it's an exhibit, it could be in-booth activities or collateral materials. If it's a date, it might be flowers or a nice restaurant.

Execute the Deliverables.

This is where you actually do the stuff. Show time. Game time. Crunch time. If you have followed The Outcome Model™ to this point, this should be the fun part.

Measure Against the Desired Outcome.

This is the easiest thing in the world, if you have clearly defined a measurable outcome. You either achieve it or you don't. This part scares some people, because they think they might measure themselves out of a job. But that's not true at all, because if you use The Outcome Model™ you always achieve your outcome.

The important thing about outcome thinking is that it is a commitment to knowing not only the steps, but how to do them… and how to make them work for you. It's an intellectual exercise, a creative exercise, an exercise in sleuthing. It is a skill that—if you master it—will become highly sought after and very lucrative for you.

So, let's give it a try!

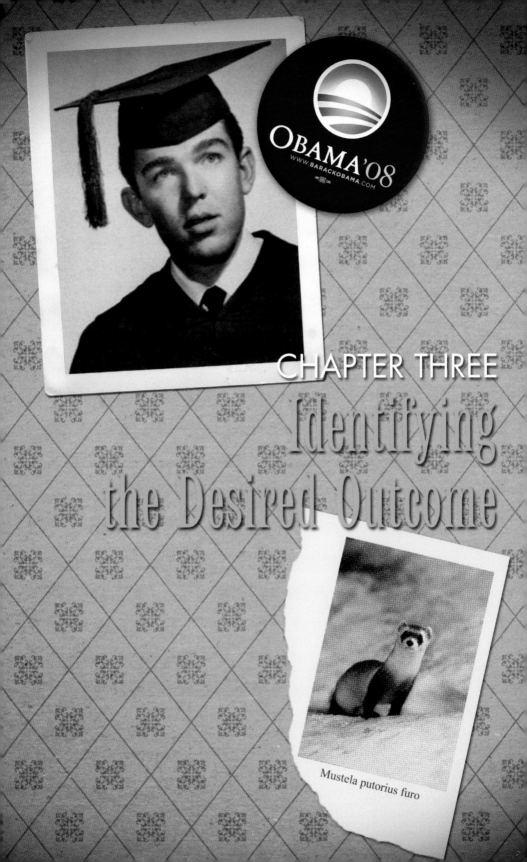

CHAPTER THREE

Identifying the Desired Outcome

Mustela putorius furo

"Simplicity is the ultimate sophistication."

- Leonardo DaVinci

Tell me what you want.

Back in 1970, my brother Spencer graduated from high school. We packed into the Ford Country Squire station wagon—my father, mother, sister, other brother, grandfather and I—and headed for the Municipal Auditorium in downtown Atlanta for the ceremony. The only time I'd been to the Municipal Auditorium before was to watch "Live Atlanta Wrestling" with my best friend Harry Angevine and his father Lyle. The feature bout was El Mongol and some guy with a skull mask. El Mongol won. I actually heard an old lady yell, "Kill him... he ain't no kin of mine!"

Anyway, the valedictorian of the North Springs High School Class of 1970 used this platform for his take on the state of society at the time. After all, it was 1970 and our nation was in turmoil. So on this warm May night, in an auditorium smelling of popcorn and perspiration, he enumerated everything he thought was wrong with American society.

It wasn't a bad speech. Notwithstanding his terrible haircut and iffy muttonchops, he was a pretty smart guy, well spoken and well organized. He made what I thought was a good case.

My grandfather wasn't quite so impressed. When the speech was over, he leaned over to me and said, "If he'd just tell me what he wants, maybe I could give it to him."

My grandfather—a man of very few words—understood that everything starts with a desired outcome. Without it, we're just flailing around aimlessly.

THE OUTCOME MODEL™ ETERNAL TRUTH
You have to be able to express what you want before you can ever begin to achieve your desired outcome.

This seems like a common sense approach, and it is. But it's not a very common process, because not many people actually do it. Some don't know how. Others simply assume that everybody's working toward the same goal already. And still others are afraid of the accountability that goes with committing to a measurable result.

What are results, really?
People talk about being results-oriented all the time. "I want results!" screams the overbearing boss while his vinyl siding salesmen cower. It's so common that it has become cliché.

You'd better do whatever it takes to "get results." For some, the obvious result is "more sales", which might seem like an adequate definition and a legitimate result. But here's where outcome thinkers earn their money!

Everybody in every business knows that the ultimate goal is to make more money. That's pretty much what you do in business. But simply identifying "more sales" as the desired outcome of doing business is like identifying "not dying on the way" as the desired outcome of visiting your sister. It's a little obvious and doesn't really "move the ball."

Outcome thinkers get down to a level where they fully understand what is relevant to the business. They understand and act on what is realistic under the current model. They explore what is possible if they change things. They focus on what can be measured specifically and reliably.

In other words, they refine, define, and state out loud what everybody else is supposedly thinking.

Assembling the Stakeholders.
And that means everybody.

Outcome thinkers are, first and foremost, outcome *mediators*, because they bring together a broad range of stakeholders and *lead* them to consensus about what is the most important, relevant, realistic, and measurable outcome for the organization.

Identifying these stakeholders is the first job.

Your knowledge of the organization will guide you in putting together the group. If you're exploring a sales-related outcome, you'll probably involve marketing, sales, product management, and operations in your group. If you're designing a new product, you'll include product designers, manufacturing engineers, maybe distribution. The makeup of the group is determined by the focus of the outcome.

Senior management needs to be involved as well.

This is particularly important when it comes to giving weight to the final decision about outcome. But in an outcome group, management has no more authority than anyone else. In fact, agreements have to be made up-front that in an outcome group, there are no managers, no supervisors, no "direct reports." There are only participants with critical knowledge unique to their positions and experiences.

You might think that a group with such widely diverse experiences, motivations, and operational focus would never be able to arrive at consensus. As the old saying goes, "a zebra is a horse built by committee." However, by its very nature, The Outcome Model™ removes superfluous paths that tend to be the result of individuals' proprietary concerns, and keeps the focus on the corporate nature of the exercise. Once members of the group understand the specificity required of the job at hand, they begin to broaden their perspectives and work quite closely together!

Let's ferret out an outcome![3]
The stakeholders—better defined as those who work for, are accountable for, and are rewarded for a corporate outcome—are the knowledge-bearers. They have your answers. If they don't have all the answers, they know where to get them. If you can lead them down the path of focused discussion on ultimate outcomes, you will have just about everything you need to be a big success.

Each stakeholder owns a particular sub-set of outcomes, which, when properly applied, managed and processed, leads to successful achievement of the overall outcome. Your job, whether you're selling a product, leading a church group, coaching a basketball team, or running a company, is to simplify this mess o' outcomes into a single focus.

> **"Everything should be made as simple as possible, but not simpler."**
> -Albert Einstein

---

[3] But first, let's check out the etymology of the phrase "ferret out." (I've always wanted to know.) To begin with, for those of you who don't keep one as a pet, the ferret is "a domesticated, usually red-eyed, and albinic variety of the polecat, used in Europe for driving rabbits and rats from their burrow"; this, according to Dictionary.com. When used as a verb, followed by the word "out," it means "to drive out by using or as if using a ferret: to *ferret rabbits from their burrows*; to *ferret out enemies*." This, also from Dictionary.com. This definition absolutely compels us to ask how one might drive out "as if" using a ferret? Maybe with an old sock filled with sand and sewed-on button eyes? I don't get it. Fortunately, Dictionary.com comes through for us in another definition, in which they define ferret (v.) as "to search out, discover, or bring to light: to *ferret out the facts*." So, now you know.

There are a number of quotations like this one. I looked and looked, but I couldn't find the source of the paraphrased sentiment that I generally offer: "Any idiot can make a problem more complicated. True genius is making it simpler." I apologize to whoever came up with that... unless it was me.

The point is, multiple perspectives from multiple stakeholders is a powerful combination when kept under control. Let it start to get away from you, and you've got Three Mile Island. Control it, and the answers begin to appear like you are reading the back page of "Cliffs Notes." Or so I have heard.

What it takes to be an outcome thinker.
This part of the process requires great listening skills and a modicum of "Oprah-esque" probing, which asks revealing questions and interprets them against your understanding of the overall context. You've got to read everybody on two levels: what they are saying professionally and what they are saying personally. That's because people live in both worlds, the personal and the professional, and in most cases they operate and make decisions somewhere in between the two.

For you to operate in this same space, you have to rely on three very important attributes: intuition, honesty, and high-level listening skills. It's the complete package of mind, body and soul!

THE OUTCOME MODEL™ ETERNAL TRUTH
Successful Outcome Thinkers have intuition, honesty, and great listening skills.

Let's take a look at these attributes one by one.

Intuition is the ability to relate what you're experiencing to everything else you've ever experienced in your life.

The fact is, you have way more value than the product you're selling or the company you represent. You have the value of all your hard work, education (scholastic and hard-knocks), experiences (good and bad), intellect (philosophical and practical), knowledge, every book you've ever read (except *The Bridges of Madison County*), every movie you've ever seen (except "The Bridges of Madison County"), every conversation you've ever engaged in, every bit of research you've ever done. Your *value* to your customer is inside your head.

Intuition is the ability to draw on all of that stuff. And it's what gives you a common bond with every person you'll ever meet. The great leaders, great sales people, great lovers, great statesmen and stateswomen, all have one thing in common. They are capable of drawing on their own life experiences to connect with others.

They can translate their recognition of similarities of motivation, process, engagement, and just plain work into a platform for helping their constituents to achieve their outcomes. You can only add value to the relationship if you can find that common ground. And you can find it by looking inside yourself.

Honesty means focusing on your customer's outcome, not yours, and using your experience, knowledge, and intellect to help him first.

The Outcome Model™ is an honest intellectual exercise, not manipulation. It's all about focusing intently on the outcome of your customer or colleague, as though you care more about that than anything else in the world right now, and then bringing your intellectual resources (and, perhaps your company's products or resources) to bear on that outcome.

When I talk about honesty, I'm not talking about telling the truth versus lying. My first boss, Bill Van Horne, told me that the most important rule of selling was the simplest: never tell a lie. So that's been ingrained in me from the beginning. What I realized as I grew in my career, however, is that there are a lot of other ways to be dishonest without telling a lie. And one of these is intellectual dishonesty.

Let me say this clearly: providing consultation to your client or colleague only for self aggrandizement is intellectually dishonest. It is no better than a surgeon insisting that you need surgery on your back just because he happens to be a surgeon. It's indefensible.[4]

Just because you sell tweezers doesn't mean that your client's sore foot is caused by a splinter. His shoes might be too tight. Intellectual honesty involves finding the answer to the question or solution to the problem as your first and foremost goal, *even if your product or serviceisn't the answer.* I promise you, this will pay off for you in the long run. In fact, as they say in Alabama, I *guaran-damn-tee* it.

Listening involves the ears first, the brain second, and the mouth almost never.

How many people do you know in business, who spend most of their time thinking about what they're going to say next? A lot of them, right?

My son, who's an anthropology major because he's not really interested in getting a job, recently had an assignment related to garbage. The professor provided a scenario in which an archeologist in the year 4077 uncovers several tightly sealed bags of garbage that are over 2,000 years old. The archeologist has to develop a theory on how many people lived in the household, their ages and sexes, their income and means of livelihood, as well as things like their personal tastes in entertainment and recreation.

By considering its contents piece by piece, he came to the conclusion that this garbage bag, which was discarded in the winter of 2005, came from a low- to middle-income single-parent family of three: one teenage boy and a female toddler and a plus-size young vegetarian mother, whose boyfriend stayed overnight only occasionally, because he was probably allergic to cats. The evidence was right there, in diapers, acne

---

[4] My golfing partner "Craze" had back surgery to repair something probably related to his football career. When the surgeon who performed it (also a former college football player) began to have the same troubles, Craze asked him when he was going to have his surgery. The surgeon said, "You think I'm gonna let one of them quacks cut on me?"

cream, magazines about vegetarianism, men's shaving products, an allergy medication, kitty litter, a nasty letter from an ex-husband, etc., etc.,
etc.

As we say in the creative business: "We don't make this stuff up." It actually comes from evidence, and in business that evidence comes from
listening. Try a little experiment on the next person who comes to sell
you something. Get into a conversation in the middle of which you in-
sert the following sentence:

> "...and I never use a real ferret, just an old sock filled
> with sand and sewed-on button eyes..."

...and then keep right on talking about the subject at hand. I will guarantee you that at least 75% of the time the salesperson will respond with
something like "uh huh," or "exactly!" or "right, right, right." Try it.

He responds this way, because he is either not paying attention or he is
madly trying to process how your eschewing a real ferret for a sand-
filled sock is going to help him sell you that Whole-Life policy.

He never for a minute considered stopping to ask: "What do you mean
by that?"

Listening is like lab work. It is how you research what your client needs
to achieve his outcome. It's the only way to help him reach his outcome.
It's part of the value you offer.

It all starts with questions.
What do you want this campaign to accomplish? What do you want
this initiative to accomplish? What do you want your company to accomplish? What do you want to accomplish? What ultimate outcome
are you looking for? Remember: your desired outcome must be realistic, specific and measurable. Here's an example:

BRUCE:	Mr. Obama, what do you want the outcome of your career to be?[5]
OBAMA:	I want to change the world.
BRUCE:	Cool. But don't you think that's a little broad?
OBAMA:	Who you calling a broad?
BRUCE:	No, I mean don't you think that's a little non-specific?
OBAMA:	Maybe, sort of, could be
BRUCE:	How would you know if you changed the world?
OBAMA:	Um. If there was peace in the Middle East.
BRUCE:	How would you know if there was peace in the Middle East?
OBAMA:	We'd sign peace treaties in both Iraq and Afghanistan.
BRUCE:	Wow.
OBAMA:	Oh, and combatants in Israel and Palestine would throw down their guns and start doing really upbeat television commercials for Dr. Pepper.
BRUCE:	Man, that would be great. But, how can a community organizer in Chicago pull that off?
OBAMA:	I guess I'd have to get elected President.
BRUCE:	Of what?
OBAMA:	The United States.
BRUCE:	"Uh-huh. Okay, what's that going to take, and how will you know you're getting there?"
OBAMA:	"Well, I guess I'd have to start by becoming an Illinois State Senator…"

And that's how I got Barack Obama elected President of the United States. Anyway, I guess you can see where I'm going with this. Indeed it does start with a vision. And it can be as grand a vision as you want it to be. But after that, the hard work starts right away. The hard work comes in parsing the vision into manageable, measurable bites. If you can manage that process with your customers, you will be their hero. Just as I was to our President. Or would have been if he'd asked.

---

[5] Simulated conversation. Do not attempt.

Parsing the vision.[6]

Don't ever let me hear you use the phrase "drilling down." It's part of that corporate-speak that I'll rail against a little later on. "Drilling down" suggests that the top layer isn't important. It is. This is more about grabbing a whole bunch of dirt and rock in a big sieve and then analyzing the components. It isn't hard; it just takes a little "ferreting" (out).

It takes understanding what the vision really means and how it might be put into everyday action. What it would look like if it was achieved. Another example:

VISION:	Achieve leadership in space.
OUTCOME:	Land a man on the moon and return him safely to the earth.
MEASURE:	Time.
SUCCESS IS:	In this decade (1960's)

If you ever want to see a great example of Outcome Thinking, rent or buy the complete mini-series "From the Earth to the Moon".[7] It's evident from the very first scene. You have a vision, a desired outcome, a way of measuring it, and then all the different things that had to happen in order to achieve it. Imagine if you could do for your customers what the guys at NASA did!

Vision.

Vision is a broad and audacious thing. It requires imagination, courage, and a willingness to take the risks necessary to achieve the vision.
In order for a vision to be realized, however, individuals within an organization must subscribe to it... and then find their role in achieving outcomes that contribute to it.

---

[6] Parse (parrs) v.—to break down into parts, explaining the form, function and interrelation of each part. This is what we used to have to do in English class, taking a sentence and breaking it down into nouns, verbs, subjects, objects, modifiers, and all that stuff. Why? So we could learn to say things like "Let's drill down and get granular."
[7] Home Box Office (1998).

Corporate role in achieving the vision.

The huge majority of people at NASA were never going to set foot in a spacecraft or push a single, solitary toggle switch in a lunar lander. But the performance of the organization as a whole would have a huge impact on whether the booster rockets would fire, the space suits would endure, or the calculations would be correct.

In this way, perfect execution of roles and processes became the focus of the "corporation" in achieving the vision. Organizationally, NASA's corporate role was to manage the processes so that everything was done right.

Individual role in achieving the vision.

The individuals in every capacity at NASA had specific roles in contributing to the achievement of the overall vision and attendant outcome. This is true in every kind of organization.

In order for people to perform at the highest level, each person needs a full understanding of where his or her work fits into the overall model and what their performance means to the achievement of the outcome.

And so we come to the inevitable pyramid required of every bona-fide business book.

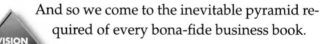

Once we understand the individual's role in achieving the vision, we can begin to itemize the outcomes that will be necessary to implement the individual's and group's contribution to the vision. If you work inside an organization, you may know a lot of the answers to these questions. Those you don't know are readily available by asking simple questions of your colleagues.

If you work outside the organization as a consultant or vendor, you should know a lot of this before every going in. If you can't find it on their web site, call your contact and ask him or her outright. From there, you should be able to determine pretty quickly where everybody fits into that corporate pursuit of a single vision.

A corporate example: managing the discovery process.
Throughout this book, I'm going to use the example of a pharmaceutical company looking for the best way to achieve its corporate vision. As you'll see, this example begins as a very broad exercise, but you'll soon learn how quickly it can become specific and measurable.[8]

Here are the particulars on this imaginary company:

Company:	GlucaWell Pharma, Inc.
Home Office:	La Jolla, California
Therapeutic Focus:	Diabetes
Key Product:	HebaC® (an oral, blood glucose–lowering drug)
Annual Sales:	$1.1 Billion
Corporate Vision:	Leadership in Diabetes Care

Because this particular organization focuses heavily on its sales and marketing organization as the primary vehicle to achievement of its vision, the group we''ll be working with is associated with sales, marketing and communications functions.

Who are the players?
To begin with, we need to understand what drives each stakeholder in his or her particular job and position within the overall enterprise.

---

[8]The pharmaceutical company I talk about throughout this book is completely fictional. None of the people or products I talk about are real. I made it all up. If you think it sounds like you, it's a coincidence.

The best way to gain this understanding is by asking questions and listening to the answers. It's important to make sure the group understands that every member is important and that every member has something important to contribute. Do not play favorites with senior management, cute members of the group or those who seem most impressed with you! Nothing good can come of sucking up to some people at the expense of losing a relationship with others. Pay attention to everyone.

So here's the lineup:

Vice President of Marketing
Female. Early 40's. Very corporate, describes herself as "driven." Advertising Agency background. Very agency oriented (prefers New York agencies because they're "more sophisticated"). Biggest issues are: reps' proper use of the new sales materials; physicians' lack of knowledge of the patient support programs; low buy-in on the physician-focused website.

Vice President of Sales
Male. About 58. Easy, likeable personality. Came from a larger pharmaceutical company with a much broader portfolio of products. Enjoys the tighter focus of this sales organization. Biggest issues are: reps' access to physicians; reps' ability to stick to the call plan (targets and frequency of calls); difficulty differentiating his products from several competitors' similar products.

Senior Product Manager
Female. Early 30's. Very passionate about her product, HebaC®. Came up through the company's field sales force. Since she's moved to the marketing side, now sees why it's important to follow the protocol for promoting products and programs. Her biggest issues: executing the marketing programs; training the sales force on the proper use of sales materials.

Senior Director–Corporate Communications

Female. Young. Responsible for meetings, conferences, trade shows, the patient call center, and a variety of internal communications initiatives. This is her first senior position in which she answers directly to the Director of Marketing, and she alternately views the product managers and the Vice President of Sales as her internal clients and/or a pain in the butt. Her biggest issue: managing all of these disparate requirements and executing whatever they decide on.

Director of Compliance

Female. 40's. Extremely knowledgeable about what can and can't be said about her products, per the FDA, and her job it is to make sure that everything the company does in promoting its products is FDA compliant. What this means is that the company and its representatives can only sell a product for the expressed purposes approved by the FDA.[9]

What did we learn?

So, here's what we've got:

1. A VP of Marketing with a high frustration level who can't understand why sales people don't see marketing materials and tools as a guide for achieving their goals.

2. A VP of Sales with many of the same issues shared by sales leaders across industries: access to the buyer, proper execution of the sales plan, proper execution of the sales call, competitive marketplace.

---

[9] For example, way back in the day, you couldn't sell Prozac® to a physician for the treatment of depression. It was only approved in the United States for the treatment of Obsessive Compulsive Disorder. That meant that even though the docs were prescribing the product for depression (that's called prescribing "off-label"), you couldn't talk about it. You could only talk about OCD. Now that Prozac® and its generics are approved for the treatment of depression, you can sell them that way.

3. A product manager who is very passionate about her product and is particularly interested in making sure that her product, promotions and programs get sufficient "face-time", because she wants her particular product to shine for management (and shareholders).

4. A Director of Communications who, in her heart, wants all of this to come together in a way that makes her company great; at the same time, she's been around long enough to know the potential minefield that a national sales meeting represents. Deep down, what she really wants is for everybody to be happy and nothing to go wrong.

5. A Director of Compliance who is there to make sure we stay on the straight and narrow with respect to our messaging. She's kind of like my wife; just do what she says, and nobody gets hurt.

THE OUTCOME MODEL™ ETERNAL TRUTH
The key to identifying an outcome is to make the problem as simple as possible, but not simpler.

While much of what these people are thinking and feeling is all over the map, a closer looks reveals that, aside from ego issues, much of what they're seeing is the same problem with a slightly different twist. Take a look:

VP of Marketing wants:
Understanding, Execution of marketing programs and processes

VP of Sales wants:
Execution of sales plan and individual calls, Effect on physicians' prescribing habits and market share growth

Product Manager wants:
Understanding, Execution of promotional materials and programs supporting her product

Director of Communications wants:
An effective and smooth-running program to achieve all of the above with no snafus
Compliance Director wants:
Us all to follow the rules

You're getting there... almost!
So, you think you had it figured out, huh? Well, bless your heart. I love you for your enthusiasm; really, I mean it. But if it was all that simple, I'd never get a book out of it. On the other hand, we've made a pretty good start from our conversations and research. And, actually, you might find that you have to probe much more to get the information that I've identified above. That's okay. You've got what everybody wants. So now, you've got to ferret out an outcome.

We've identified some of the motivations and goals of our group of pharmaceutical executives, and we've tried to simplify them into common words and phrases that have meaning for the entire group. So, let's pretend we're looking at one of those irritating flip charts pages taped to the wall.

Understand marketing programs.
Execute processes.
Get more access to docs.
Understand the promotional materials.
Execute each sales call properly.
Change docs prescribing habits.
Increase Market Share for UebaC(r) by 3 points
Get buy in on Docs2Us.com
On time! Under budget!
No off-label promotion!!!!
Follow the sales plan
~~Broad collaboration among teams with synergies~~
Represent our company the way you should
Use the Master Sales Aid!
Provide all this information effectively to field
Be a team-player and have passion!!!

Separating outcomes from behaviors.

Okay, you've got the very first list of "outcomes" that your group of executives has provided you. Now it's time to earn your money. Let's quickly review what an outcome has to be: realistic, specific, and measurable.

The one that usually trips people up is "Measurable." So, let's start by eliminating those that aren't immediately measurable through existing indices and/or specific enough to track.

We tried to save a couple of these suggestions by being more specific, as you can see. But it's really important, if you want to get down to the nitty-gritty of outcome thinking, that you separate legitimate outcomes from behaviors. It may be a subtle difference, but it can be critical to measurability. A quick baseball example might help here: a home run is a behavior, while a run

~~Understand marketing programs.~~
~~Execute processes.~~
Get more access to docs.
~~Understand the~~ promotional materials. use properly
Execute each sales call properly
Change docs prescribing habits.
Increase Market Share for UebaC(r) by 3 points
Get buy in on Docs2Us.com
~~On time! Under budget!~~
No off-label promotion!!!!
Follow the sales plan
~~Broad collaboration among teams with synergies~~
~~Represent our company the way you should~~
Use the Master Sales Aid! AS TRAINED!
Provide all this information effectively to field
~~Be a team-player and have passion!!!~~

on the scoreboard is an outcome. You want a certain number of players on your team to engage in this behavior so you can achieve the outcome of scoring more runs than the other team.

THE OUTCOME MODEL™ ETERNAL TRUTH
Identifying a desired outcome requires separating outcomes from behaviors.

As you'll see in the next chapter, the second step of The Outcome Model™ process is identifying behaviors that have to change in order to achieve the desired outcome. The outcome needs to be something that is almost impersonal, almost mathematical.

Staying away from behaviors for our outcomes is important, because it helps us to avoid broad, overarching, and generally subjective measures.

If you look at the chart, you'll see that one of the things we wrote down was "Use the master sales aid as trained." Even though this is specific, it speaks to individual execution of one of the sales competencies, rather than one of the corporate outcomes we're looking for. We're going to cross it off, because it is a change in behavior that will help us achieve the ultimate outcome. It's not an ultimate outcome itself.

So, let's look again and see which of our supposed outcomes is the least animate. Or, at least let's remove those that have to do with specific behaviors, since we'll get to them next.

You'll notice we cross things out lightly, because we may need them

48

later under the behaviors category. Except that one about "synergies." We knocked that out right off the bat because we don't engage in Corporate Speak anymore, right?

With these changes, we have started to identify the key outcomes that will contribute to the overall vision of the company, and that we can communicate, measure and understand what has to take place for them to be realized.

But they're still not specific enough, so let's put them on another piece of that infernal flip chart paper, tape it to the wall, and get those executives working again! They're having fun now, because they know there's a payoff at the end. That's what's great about engaging people in this exercise, because not only are they interacting with you, but they are involved in a business exercise rather than a buying exercise.

Get more access to docs.

Change docs prescribing habits.

Increase Market Share for UebaC(r) by 3 points

Get buy in on Docs2Us.com

We'll start with the four outcomes that are left, as they were originally written. It's important that we fully understand what each member of our group meant when he or she offered their original outcomes. As we

49

said at the beginning, this is not a pedantic exercise. It's a relationship, and it requires continued engagement of each and every player.

The fact that some of the suggestions didn't make the final cut only means that many of them have provided you with answers to Step 2 of the process, changes in behavior. Keep this out in front of them, so they know it and continue to buy in. If they offer a suggestion which more appropriately belongs in another step of the process, explain exactly where their suggestion fits, and make sure that they see how valuable each step is.

Let me give you a specific example. The Vice President of Marketing, who is frustrated anyway (and, by her own definition, "driven") can't be very happy that you have crossed out her first offering: "Understand all marketing programs." In fact, you've just given her reason to cross you off her list of vendors (you're not even from New York), unless you can act quickly to dispel her notion that you've just dissed her. Let's play out this little scenario.

YOU: So, we're going to cross out "understand all marketing programs as a little broad."

HER: Who are you calling a little broad?

YOU: No, what I mean is, we'll take that outcome out of the mix because it's not quite specific enough to be a measurable outcome.

HER: What do you mean we can't measure it? It's the most important thing to driving sales in the next five years. Our reps have to understand our marketing programs in order to be able to promote our products. I don't think you've done enough research about our company. Where are you from?

YOU: Actually, what I mean to say by that is this: it is absolutely critical that the field sales organization understands not only the programs themselves, but the strategy behind them, so that they can see how this comprehensive strategy supports their day-to-day field selling activities.

HER: That's what I said.

YOU: Exactly. But the reason it's not an outcome per se is that your programs actually create the context for their activities in the field. We can't even think about OUTCOMES before they are well-versed in the program. I thought that would go without saying.

HER: It certainly does.

YOU: Indeed. And, that's why you'll find it at the top of the list of "Changes In Behavior Necessary to Achieving the Outcome." There's no sense even talking about outcomes if they're not fluent in the programs.

HER: Agreed.

YOU: Please forgive me for assuming that went without saying.

HER: It does.

YOU: Exactly.

Phew, that was close. You next statement should be something like, "and we'll be getting to those critical changes in behavior in just a couple of minutes. I hope you'll help me with that."

Of course she will. Because you've already sensed that she doesn't think the field sales force knows their ass from a hole in the ground, and she'll be more than willing to offer up changes in sales-force behavior 'til the cows come home. In fact, she's making notes right now. And I don't mean to make light of this. You knew from the start that this particular executive was going to test you and "push back" (as they say), so it should come as no surprise to you that she'll challenge you. You'd better be ready.

Refining the outcomes.

So, now that you've averted that disaster, you can return to the flip chart and begin to refine the outcomes. Every round of our little game should result in more specific and more measurable outcomes. You've pretty much done the hard part, and now you're counting on your client to provide most of the answers.

Ultimately, what you're looking for is an agreed-upon definition of each outcome, parameters within which that outcome is considered achieved, and means of measuring success.

QUESTION: How do you define "more access to docs"?
First of all, what's access? A quick hello? A trip through the master sales aid? A willingness for the physician to talk to you? A willingness for a physician to talk about a specific product or clinical reprints? For how long?

ANSWER: Access to a targeted physician is defined as the willingness of the physician to meet with a rep face-to-face to review either the Master Sales Aid or a clinical reprint.

QUESTION: How do you define "more"? Is that more than zero? Seeing the same docs more times? Does it mean finding more docs to see?

ANSWER: "More" access to docs means an increase in the actual number of targeted physicians who have not met with us over these materials before, and who agree to meet with us over these materials now.

In this case, sales management has identified the targeted physicians for each territory. That's part of the sales plan (remember "Follow the sales plan" from the original sheet of outcomes?), so it will be easy to measure how many targeted physicians who haven't met with a rep in the past will be willing to meet with a rep now.

QUESTION: How many is "more," and do you have a time frame in which you want this outcome achieved?

ANSWER: We would like to increase our access to physicians by 25% in the next three months. That means, nationwide, we will have to meet with 1,475 targeted physicians with whom we have not met before. Our data show that approximately 35% of those who see this information prescribe the product to at least one patient within the first three months.

By the end of Q2, share the Master Sales Aid with 1,475 Targeted Physicians who have not previously seen them. (25% increase)

By the end of Q2, share the Clinical Reprint with 1,475 Targeted Physicians who have not previously seen them. (25% increase)

Increase market share for UebaC(r) by 3 points by the end of the fiscal year

Increase number of physicians registered on Doc2Us.com to 5,000 by end of Q3. (20% increase)

It's important to notice how specific these candidates for desired outcome have become. We have specified the successful mission and the time frame. We have said we want at least 1,475 "new" docs detailed on the product information by the end of the new quarter. We have said we want a market share increase of three points by the end of the year, and so on.

The final cut: Outcome vs. behavior.
You'll discover that three of the four items listed here are actually very specific *behaviors* that will lead to the achievement of the ultimate outcome. Everyone in the group agrees. In order to achieve a 3-point

growth in market share, it will be necessary to share the materials described with the physicians. The ultimate outcome is the 3-point-share growth.

By the end of Q2, share the Master Sales Aid with 1,475 ~~BEHAVIOR~~ sicians who have not previously seen them. (25% increase)

By the end of Q2, share the Clinical Reprint with 1,475 Targeted Ph~~BEHAVIOR~~ns who have not previously ~~BEHAVIOR~~ (25% increase)

Increase market share for UebaC(r) by 3 points by the end of the fiscal year

Increase number of physicians registered on Doc2Us.com to 5,000 by end of Q3. (20% increase)

BEHAVIOR

This is the most subtle and difficult distinction that you will ultimately learn how to make. If it is an action you can control, it is a behavior. If it is a result of an action, it is an outcome. You'll often find in your discovery process, that you almost automatically identify necessary behaviors at the same time you're identifying your ultimate desired outcome. And that's what you've done here.

We finally have a clear description of our desired outcome. It's relevant, because it supports the vision of leadership in the therapeutic area. It's realistic, because this level of share growth is achievable in this industry. And it's measurable, because we have committed to a specific number within a specific time frame.

We're no different from NASA! We're going to the moon! And we've just set the stage for the next step of our Outcome Model™, where we'll determine what we will actually need to change in order to achieve these outcomes.

	NASA APOLLO PROGRAM	PHARMACEUTICAL COMPANY
VISION	Leadership in Space	Leadership in Diabetes Care
DESIRED OUTCOME	Land a man on the moon and return him safely to the earth before 1970	Increase market share for Product A by 3 points by end of fiscal year

CHAPTER FOUR

Changing
Audience Behavior

"Mankind will possess...extraordinary control over human behavior...when the human mind will contemplate itself not from within but from without."

- Ivan Petrovich Pavlov[10]

The second step of the Outcome Model™ is the most fun. We get to ask ourselves: Just what changes in behavior will have to take place in order for us to achieve the outcomes we've identified?

You mean we get to change people's behavior? You bet! And, we'll discover along the way, that we get to change ours, too.

Oh, you skeptics. I can hear you now: "I told my mother I could change the way my husband lies around the house and doesn't lift a finger to help me, and that was 25 years ago. She never got to see it, rest her soul."

Notwithstanding the fact that you were a disappointment to your poor, departed mother, The Outcome Model™ and Outcome Communications™ rely entirely on effecting certain critical changes. Defined outcomes are nothing but fantasies until changes are attached to put them into action. That's why they call it work!

Pavlov was right. It is only when we make the behavior like any other natural phenomenon, that is, measurable, reportable, and "subject to external analysis"[11], that we can develop a program for achieving our outcomes. This means behaviors aren't about doing right and wrong;

---

[10] Yes, the salivating dog guy. I mean, the guy with salivating dogs. From Scientific Study of So-Called Psychical Processes in the Higher Animals [1906].
[11] Ibid.

they're about doing what is necessary to achieve an expressed outcome. Behaviors are about taking steps, and changing behavior starts with the individual.

Again, we need to separate the outcome from the individual behavior.

THE OUTCOME MODEL™ ETERNAL TRUTH
Outcomes are corporate, while change in behavior always starts with the individual.

Our job is to identify these necessary changes. Everybody's heard the old joke about the doctor who asks his patient, "does it hurt when you do this?" And when the patient says yes, the doctor says, "Well don't do that." It's pretty simple.

This is just the obverse of that. Doc says "do you feel better when you do this?" Patient says yes, and doc says, "Then do it!"

Crusty old baseball coach example.
Let's walk my old high school baseball coach[12] through the Outcome Model.™

The vision for any baseball coach is to win the pennant. That breaks down to a series of winning games, divisions, leagues, and, of course, whatever championship series or game will result in the ultimate championship. So the vision is out there.

The objectives can be easily identified and easily measured, given that baseball is probably the most statistically analyzed sport on the planet. You have to throw the ball, hit the ball, and catch the ball in a manner in which you achieve outs against the other guys and runs for yourself.

The ultimate desired outcome of every single game is to score more runs

---

[12] This coach " 'splained" baseball thusly: "It's simple, boys. You got a round bat and a round ball. All you gotta do is hit it square".

Achieve a team earned run average under 3.5

Achieve a team batting average of over .300

Achieve a team fielding percentage of over .996

by the end of the 9th inning than the other team. Now, obviously, the ultimate desired outcome will be affected by the quality of throwing, catching and hitting that you do. So, if you take care of achieving measurable outcomes in each of these areas, the score is likely to take care of itself. (Just like "more sales" will result from achieving other specific and measurable outcomes.)

So, the outcomes for a baseball coach generally focus on those three areas: pitching, hitting, and fielding. Let's look at one of those flip chart sheets for the coach. These measurable outcomes are very specific and ambitious.[13] They relate to pitching as measured by earned run average,

---

[13] In 2008, the best Major League Baseball team earned run average (runs per 9-innings not caused by fielding errors) was 3.49; the best team batting average (hits/at-bats) was.289; the best team fielding percentage (non-error plays/chances) was .989.

hitting as measured by batting average, and fielding as measured by fielding percentage.

Of course, ultimately, the winners score more runs than their opponents, and none of these statistics in and of itself is a guarantor of victory, any more than the perfect sales person doing all the right things is a guarantee you'll reach your sales goals. But, we control the things we can control, and there are certain behaviors that will improve our chances dramatically.

Be specific!
There are a number of behaviors that are necessary, if you're going to achieve a high batting average. You've heard them: they include things like keeping your eye on the ball, swinging level, turning your hips at the right time... all that stuff they want you to remember as a golfer, too. Which means it's not as easy as it sounds.

When I was playing baseball "back in the day," I was a good overall hitter. What I had trouble with, though, was the inside pitch. If the pitcher could get it in on my hands, I was always hitting it off my fists (the handle of the bat), which inevitably resulted in a weak grounder and an easy out. Turns out, many of the guys on my team had the same weakness; so the coach suggested some changes to our batting approach, and our team average rose dramatically. That is an effective change in behavior.

Here's the secret. He told me to stand as far away from the plate as I could get while still being able to reach to the far front corner of the plate. What this meant was that I could reach a ball on the outside corner, but I had plenty of room on the inside corner to get the fat part of the bat on the ball. Any pitch that "jammed" me was going to be a ball anyway, and I didn't have to swing at it. I hit a hundred points higher after that little tip!

In many cases, that's how specific we have to get with changes in behavior in order to have those changes affect the outcome. We don't say "try harder," "be more passionate," or "be a better hitter." We don't say, "try harder," "be more passionate," "sell smarter," or "be more professional." We provide guidance to change specific behaviors that will have a positive impact on the desired outcome.

Let's compare examples again:

	NASA APOLLO PROGRAM	BASEBALL TEAM
VISION	Leadership in Space	Championship
DESIRED OUTCOME	Land a man on the moon and return him safely to the earth before 1970	Improve team batting average to .300 by the end of the season
CHANGE IN BEHAVIOR NECESSARY TO ACHIEVE DESIRED OUTCOME		Move batters away from plate to improve access to inside pitch

Now let's try a sales example. Going back to GlucaWell Pharma, Inc., we'll now have to engage in a discussion about what behaviors must change in order to achieve their desired outcomes.

Take a look at the outcome they identified that will have the greatest individual effect on the bottom line: "Increase Market Share for HebaC® by 3 points by the end of the fiscal year".

Know who the audience is.

Here's where we return to our pyramid to be reminded of our focus. Before we ask what changes in behavior need to take place, let's review who our audience is. Because, not only the outcomes, but the actions required to achieve those outcomes have to reflect the individual role in achieving the corporate vision. While the outcomes are corporate, the changes in behavior start with the individual.

63

In this case, we will be communicating in some fashion to the field sales organization. So we'll be focusing on changes in behavior in this specific audience of field sales representatives, district managers, and regional managers.

When we ask our group of executives, we find that they approach this problem from several different angles. Let's take a look at what they're saying:

VP of Marketing: "This is all about competency with the marketing strategy. They need to understand where our product fits in the treatment algorithm and why we market the way we do."

VP of Sales: "Having something new to tell these physicians is the key. They see us when they can learn something new."

Product Manager: "They need to present the Master Sales Aid and clinical reprint correctly for this to have any effect on their prescribing habits."

Director of Communications: "This is all about training. They have to be competent to present the materials. We have to train them to that competency level."

So, what do you say here? You may sound like a broken record, but what's good for the outcome is good for the behavior change:

THE OUTCOME MODEL™ ETERNAL TRUTH
The behavior change must be relevant, realistic and measurable.

That's right. Just like the outcome, we have to identify behavior changes that can be achieved, are clear and concise so as to be easily understood, and that can be measured.

What do we learn from all this talking? What behaviors need to be changed in order to achieve the desired outcome? Let's take a look at one of the broader statements made by a member of the team. I'm going to take the hardest one.

"This is all about competency with the marketing programs. They need to understand where our product fits in the treatment algorithm and why we market the way we do."
-VP of Marketing

It's easy to make broad statements about behaviors we expect of people we know. Just the other day, my son told me a friend was joining him on a road trip he was making to take a girl to her law school dance. "Mac," his friend, was going to be a blind date for the girl's roommate. I know Mac. Here's what I said:

"Do you think Mac can act right?"

What did I mean by this? Well, down south, "acting right" means something about being a gentleman, showing your best manners, approaching the situation with prudence, good sense, as though your mama was looking over your shoulder. But in the larger world, and when applied to specific outcomes, it doesn't mean much at all. And, unfortunately, as managers, we often resort to this kind of shorthand version of direction when communicating with our troops.

Here's one I heard not too long ago.

"The success of this program will depend entirely on your commitment to be the people you can be."

I don't think so. I mean, we all want to be the people we can be... we all want to be "An Army of One" (I guess), but to spend one red cent on delivering a "be all you can be" message to your own employees as a focalpoint of your behavior model suggests that you have either hired the wrong employees or you've got the wrong guy on stage delivering the message.

People we pay generally want to "act right." Most of them are committed to "being the people they can be." But after that, to paraphrase my grandfather from all those years ago, you've got to "tell them what you want, and maybe they can give it to you!"

Here's an example of how to do that:

"Mac, stay sober and keep your paws off the girl."

Now there's a message he could understand! This is first and foremost about identifying those behaviors that will help your audience achieve the outcomes you've outlined. Then you can build your message around those changes in behavior. Let's start by practicing how we can glean these ideal behaviors and define them concisely so that they are specific and measurable.

Start by rewriting or restating what they say.
The best way to start is to take the statements made by your team of executives and rewrite them as imperatives. You'll find that most people talk in multiples, saying two or three things in every "single" statement they make. So it helps to ferret out(!) what is useful. We'll start with our VP of Marketing. Here's her statement again, but we've highlighted some key words that will lead us either to ask additional questions or to reorganize the comment.

> "This is all about competency with the marketing programs. They need to understand where our product fits in the treatment algorithm and why we market the way we do."

Oh, boy. There's a lot going on in there. Let's take a look at the individual words or phrases first. Here they are:

"Competency with the marketing programs"
"Where our product fits into the treatment algorithm"
"Why we market the way we do"

Now, let's rewrite them as imperatives.

"Execute our marketing programs."

"Show where our product fits into the treatment algorithm."

"Understand the marketing strategy."

As you can see, this is all still pretty general stuff. We need some specific answers about how each of these is behavior-related, how the behavior needs to be changed, and what kind of effect these changes will have on the overall desired outcome. So, let's direct some questions to our VP of Marketing, focusing on the first imperative, "Execute our marketing strategy."

What are the key marketing programs that apply directly to the sales process?

How do these programs affect how a sales person gains access to any targeted physician, especially one who has not been detailed before?

How do these programs affect how a sales person influences and changes a doctor's prescribing habits?

What defines competency in the execution of these specific programs?

We will ask the same kinds of questions about each of these imperatives, in order to determine what needs to happen, what needs to change, and why.

You'll find this to be a several-step process.

Here are the answers given to us by our VP of Marketing. You'll see that we are making progress in the discovery process, because we're becoming much more specific than before. Watch it work:

What are the key marketing programs that apply directly to the sales process?

The new Master Sales Aid, the Clinical Reprint, our new website, Docs2Us.com, and our new exhibit.

How do programs affect how a sales person gains access to any targeted physician, especially one who has not been detailed before?

The new Master Sales Aid will provide physicians with new clinical data and a more on-target message for their patients.

Our reprint provides a solid clinical foundation for our product story, along with the science a physician needs.

Our proprietary web site, Docs2Us.com, allows us to remain top-of-mind with physicians who use it for the support services it provides.

Our new exhibit will give us a much larger presence at the major medical meetings, where these docs are.

How do these programs affect how a sales person influences and changes a doctor's prescribing habits?

Prescribing habits are changed by calling on the right physicians the right number of times. These components give us a story to tell, clinical information to back it up, a resource that physicians need to help their patients, and a way to reach physicians maybe for the first time.

What defines competency in the execution of these specific programs?

Each one is different.

Now ask "How?"

Excellent. Now we're getting down to the nitty-gritty. So we ask the question, how? What behaviors represent competency in each of these areas, and how can we measure them? Suddenly we find ourselves talking about actual behaviors that need to change in order for us to achieve our desired outcomes.

Master Sales Aid

Behavior: Achieve proficiency in delivering the Master Sales Aid messaging by the end of the upcoming National Sales Meeting.

Measurement: Pass written competency and role-play tests.

Clinical Reprint

Behavior: Achieve proficiency in delivering the information contained in the Clinical Reprint by the end of the National Sales Meeting.

Measurement: Pass written competency and role-play tests.

MSA and Clinical Reprint

Behavior: Share the new MSA and/or Clinical Reprint with 50% of your targeted doctors by the end of Q1.

Measurement: Number of presentations vs. number of targets.

New Website

Behavior: Personally deliver Docs2Us.com info sheet and quick-sign-up authorization card to 100% of your non-registered physician targets by the end of Q1.

Measurement: Offers vs. number of unregistered targets.

New Exhibit

Behavior: Achieve an "A" grade on all exhibit assignments: training sessions, off-site events, and work hours. Follow exhibit protocol for interacting with and selling to all visitors.

<u>Measurement:</u> District or Regional Manager report cards.

Pretty good stuff, huh? Now each individual in the audience knows what he or she needs to do with regard to the marketing programs that pertain to them. So, let's check our progress so far.

	ClucaWell Pharma	MEASURABLE?
VISION	Leadership in Therapeutic Area	
OUTCOME	Increase HebaC® Market Share by 3%	👍
CHANGE IN BEHAVIOR	Achieve proficiency in delivering Master Sales Aid messaging by the end of upcoming National Sales Meeting	👍
CHANGE IN BEHAVIOR	Achieve proficiency in delivering Clinical Reprint information by the end of upcoming National Sales Meeting	👍
CHANGE IN BEHAVIOR	Share new MSA and/or Clinical Reprint with 50% of targeted physicians by end of Q1	👍
CHANGE IN BEHAVIOR	Personally deliver Docs2Us.com info sheet and quick-sign-up authorization card to 100% of non-registered targets by end of Q1	👍
CHANGE IN BEHAVIOR	Achieve "A" grade on all exhibit assignments	👍

General knowledge improves intuition.
Before I go on, I want to talk about a very subtle, yet very important nuance about outcome thinking. We can see almost immediately that that knowledge of the overall marketing strategy, unlike the other two, doesn't have a measurable or direct impact on the outcome. At least not to the naked eye.

However, this knowledge provides a critical context for talking about everything else. A pharmaceutical sales rep is not going to be asked what the company's marketing strategy is, at least by a doctor prescribing his or her product! But, this general knowledge simply makes the sales rep smarter and promotes his or her buy-in to the specific marketing elements he or she will be asked to execute.

General knowledge, like the liberal arts, gives a person perspective. Perspective is a part of professional intuition. We talked about it a few chapters back. Remember what we said about intuition? **Intuition is the ability to relate what you're experiencing to everything else you've ever experienced in your life.** It's a function of what you know. The more you know, the greater your intuition. That's why we're leaving it in, and that's why it's one of our eternal truths.

THE OUTCOME MODEL™ ETERNAL TRUTH
People who have a broad base of general knowledge are better at applying The Outcome Model™ than those who do not.

You can totally take that to the bank, because when it comes down to a dog fight, the smarter dog's going to win just about every time. And that knowledge–combined with a clear understanding of the desired and expected outcome, as well as the behaviors required to achieve it–creates the pathway to success for yours or anybody else's company in the world. Now all we have to do is communicate it so everybody understands it and execute it so everybody achieves it!

CHAPTER FIVE

Defining
the Core Message

"Talk doesn't cook rice."

-Chinese Proverb

It should be apparent by now that every step of The Outcome Model™ is driven by a purpose, and that purpose is to cause people to take effective actions to achieve desired outcomes. Creating a core message is the starting point for communicating what these effective actions are.

This takes time, and time must be spent.
Our executive team at GlucaWell Pharma is all excited now, because we're getting close to the "prize". But it's taken a while; probably more than just one meeting or a couple of conference calls. To get to this point many of our executives may have had to consult with their own teams or simply spend some time thinking about it.

I'm sure it comes as no surprise to you that a lot of people in business want simple solutions to even the most complex questions. It may have something to do with this new culture of instant gratification, and it's probably safe to blame the whole thing on video games. The executives you're working with are likely to be a little bit impatient to get this far in The Outcome Model™ or any other extended thought process for that matter. That's because they were never made to adhere to the "Eat the Cereal to Get to The Prize Paradigm."

I don't know about you, but back in the early '60s, my mother made us actually eat the cereal before we got to the prize. I'd like to say this made discovery of the prize more satisfying, but it didn't. It just made it take longer.[14]

This is one of your challenges as an Outcome Communications™ professional. You have to find a way to keep these very important folks engaged in the process throughout.

Interestingly, I think you'll find that higher-level executives are generally more willing to commit to the exercise than others. There are several reasons for this. As a rule, higher-level executives have greater access to corporate strategies and a broader knowledge of desired outcomes. In their jobs, they can also "give themselves permission" to think on this level rather than be merely involved in "fulfillment" of the final product.

I have often found that some mid-level executives are much more task oriented, and they are not as quick to look beyond achievement of the task as their desired outcome. You might ask a corporate communications manager what her desired outcome is for a communications piece, and she might say "get it done on schedule without any screw-ups." Of course this really has nothing to do with the outcome of the piece itself, but rather the completion of the task.

But I will say this. The Outcome Model™ is a relationship exercise, not a mere business "process." And the heart of success in any relationship exercise (including selling or managing) will always be **authenticity.**

---

[14] I'm lying. We never got the kind of cereal that had a prize in it. We got shredded wheat. Not the little bite-sized ones, but the big ones that you had to tear up like a square of sod before you could choke it down. This is why I am not a people-person. If I'd gottenFroot Loops, I'd have a sunnier disposition. The point is, if Mom had let us have Frosted Flakes, she'd have certainly made us eat our way down to the prize rather than going elbow-deep to pull it out. By the way, after years of therapy I'm "this close" to forgiving her.

How authentic are you in your interest, your questions, your conclusions, your work toward an outcome, your relationship with these people?

Your level of authenticity will directly affect how successful you are in becoming their resource for achieving outcomes, finding solutions, bettering their businesses, and fulfilling their needs as clients, colleagues, and associates. You have to be doing what you're doing *for the good of the people you are serving.* Believe me, they'll know if you're doing it just for you. And they won't like that at all.

Here are some business-book-like pointers for being authentic:

1. **ACCEPT** – that their success is a measure of yours

2. **UNDERSTAND** – their jobs, their lives, their challenges

3. **TREAT** – them as real people; have real conversations

4. **HELP** – is your product; give it away freely

5. **ENTHUSE** – over their great ideas, and don't fake it!

6. **NOTICE** – everything; it all has meaning

7. **THINK** – long and hard; it's what you're paid for

8. **INTUIT** – from your experiences to their benefit

9. **CARE** – about their outcomes with all your heart

The fact that I used all the letters of the word *AUTHENTIC* is cheesy–there's no denying it. However, if you do every one of these things all the time, you will be the most successful professional in the history of your company, industry, and very possibly the world. Think of the best person you ever met. Wouldn't you want him or her contributing to your success? When you're authentic, you *are* the best person most people have ever met.

It's time to communicate with our audience.
It's only after identifying desired outcomes and necessary behavior changes that we begin to formulate what and how we are going to communicate our directives to our audience. Remember in my golfing example how the whole process began with a question? As we stood on the tee, Ed asked, "What kind of putt do you want?" He didn't tell me what or how to do anything. And he certainly didn't make any suggestions about where I should drive the ball (assuming I had any control over that to begin with!).[15]

Lewis Carroll said it very well: "Take care of the sense, and the sounds will take care of themselves."[16] We should consider this as a guiding statement. In fact, thank you, Lewis.

THE OUTCOME MODEL™ ETERNAL TRUTH
Take care of the sense, and the sounds will take care of themselves.

I guess I should really say, "Thank you, Charles," because Lewis Carroll is actually the pseudonym of the English mathematician Charles Lutwidge Dodgson who, in addition to writing fantastical stories about white rabbits and mad hatters was a logician and lecturer on mathematics at Christ Church College, Oxford. He also wrote guides for students. Lewis Carroll was an historic outcome thinker!

For the past 30 years, I've been involved in "corporate communications" in one form or another. When I first started, I was absolutely positive that corporate communications was all about"coming up with the big

---

[15] Don't you hate those guys in the gallery who yell "in the hole!" when a guy tees off on a five par? It's just stupid. It's also why they shouldn't serve beer at golf tournaments.
[16] *Alice's Adventures in Wonderland* (1865).

idea. " You know, sort of like Darrin Stephens trying to come up with a new campaign for the "Rover-Rex Dog Food Account" without Samantha's help. All this while Larry had an anxiety attack and another martini.[17]

I no longer live under this misapprehension, and it has made my life a lot easier. The fact is, it isn't my job to come up with "the big idea." It's my job to facilitate the *effective communication of the connection between certain actions and outcomes.* This is eminently more realistic and more profitable, as dull as it may sound. Just remember, curling is an Olympic sport, and their gold medals are just as big as the ones for downhill skiing.

I realize this isn't nearly as much "fun" as making something up out of the ether of synapse and chemical reaction. On the other hand, it's way less likely to make you look like a fool. Let me give you some examples from my storied career:

- The marketing director of a penile implant company wanted to use Judy Garland's image to promote his "A Star is Born" campaign for a new product that pumps up "automatically."

- The head of a banking institution wanted to celebrate his company's most profitable year with a campaign called "Is It a Dream or Is It Reality?"

- A pharmaceutical sales manager decided to recognize his high performing reps as exclusive members of "The Cheetah Club," because their product logo was a cheetah. Of course the Cheetah Club is a well-known chain of strip clubs across the United States, featuring a different kind of "performance" than he probably had in mind.

---

[17] You know, Samantha could have improved Darrin's life by simply conjuring up a way to banish Larry to the netherworld and install Darrin as the head of the advertising agency. That way they could have had a better house and bought a condo for Endora in Boca. Also, I wonder why she never noticed that the Darrin she ended up with wasn't the same Darrin she started out with. You'd think a witch would notice something like that.

- A chain of all-you-can-eat buffet restaurants selected an advertising tag line which proudly asked, "When's it gonna hit ya?"[18]

Okay now, granted, it's easy to throw stones. But here are four examples of messages that did *not* deliver to outcomes. I think the closest to on-target was the all-you-can-eat buffet, but certainly not for the reason they were thinking of.

They all miss the mark–and miss it by lightyears–because they don't reflect the core messages these businesses want to convey

Let's start with what a Core Message really is.

THE OUTCOME MODEL™ ETERNAL TRUTH
The Core Message is a brief and straightforward way to communicate the connection between actions and outcomes.

The Core Message is brief, straightforward, and makes the critical connection between the behavior and the result. The Core Message *is not* a theme or a tag line. In fact, you have to understand your Core Message, which represents the logic supporting a program or campaign, before you create a pithy, marketable tag for it.

I think Nike is one of the greatest examples in the world of a company that has used outcome thinking to change the way the consumer behaves. If we take Nike athletic shoes as an example, we know that it was Nike's vision to be the worldwide leader in athletic shoes. Their desired outcome therefore was to achieve a certain identified share of the athletic shoe market.

The change in consumer behavior necessary to achieve this outcome was both clear and measurable. The consumer would have to buy more Nike product. But there was a deeper behavioral change that had to take place, too, and we've certainly seen evidence of it over the past two

---

[18] Choose the chicken-fried steak, and it's "gonna hit ya" right about NOW.

decades. People needed to connect the brand with the successful achievement of a personal goal.

The consumer's behavior had to reflect the following beliefs:

"Being fit is good and good looking."
"I have to exercise to be fit."
"Nike is a good and good-looking way to exercise."

So there's the core message: "Nike is the good and good-looking way to get fit and good looking." It tied the behavior change to the desired outcome for both the consumer and the company.

All kinds of companies have since followed Nike's lead in delivering the same basic Core Message. All you have to do is watch TV to see it over and over again. From sports drinks to sportswear to diet plans to fitness clubs, they all make that connection between using their product and getting "good looking."

But nobody ever tied a tag line to it as well as Nike did: "Just Do It." It's the simplest and most broadly evocative statement in advertising history. It says everything there is to say about you, the choices you make, the products you desire, the things you want your life to be, and the outcomes you're willing to commit to. "Just Do It." It's almost a biblical imperative! It's practically the eleventh commandment!

I believe an entire generation of consumers changed the way they thought and acted, simply because Nike wanted to achieve a certain market share number.[19] Now *that's* Outcome Communications™!

So how do we achieve this same kind of success in identifying our Core Message and leveraging it to deliver behaviors which ultimately result in achieving desired outcomes?

---

[19] In 2008, Nike achieved an astounding all-time high market share of nearly 50% in the U.S. footwear market..

First and foremost, we need to see the Core Message as a *business message*, not as a promotional message. We'll have plenty of time to deliver the marketing and panache later on, but right now we want to make sure the business message is clear.

THE OUTCOME MODEL™ ETERNAL TRUTH

The Core Message is a business message, not a promotional message.

Start with the most rudimentary expression of the message.
If we're saying we want our sales representatives to adhere to the sales plan we have developed for them, because to do so will increase their chances of achieving stated sales goals, we need to state that as simply as possible.

I recently had a client describe his Core Message thusly: "Work the *&$!#@&* plan!" Well, he certainly gets points for making his message brief and straightforward. What it lacks, of course, is the all-important connection between the behavior and a desired outcome.

I would venture to say the implied message is something along the lines of "work the plan and you won't be killed." But we're not dealing in the currency of implied messages here. We're looking for something much more substantive to trade on. Perhaps a better way to express it would be "Work the *&$!#@&* plan, and the *&$!#@&* plan will work for you."

All kidding aside, the straightforward connection between the behavior and the outcome will make all kinds of things simpler for you, as you'll see in subsequent chapters. A good Core Message will practically write its own copy, produce its own commercial spots, create its own tag lines and sell its own deliverables. You'll see.

"If you build it, he will come." Simple, straightforward, and effective.

So, what is our "if you build it, he will come" core message for GlucaWell Pharma? Let's take a look.

Let's go back to the outcome and behavior change. That's how we're going to know how to express the connection between the two.

The outcome our group identified was to increase HebaC®, market share by three percentage points. It is relevant to their business, realistic (according to their market research), and measurable. They identified several changes in audience behavior that would be necessary to achieve this outcome. They were:

- Achieve proficiency in delivering Master Sales Aid messaging
- Achieve proficiency in delivering Clinical Reprint information
- Share new MSA and/or Clinical Reprint with 50% of target physicians by the end of the first quarter
- Personally deliver the Docs2Us.com information sheet and quick-sign-up authorization card to 100% of non-registered targets by the end of the first quarter

The first two changes in behavior are all about knowing how to deliver the information correctly. The last two changes are directly related to the delivery of the message to targeted prospects. Each is critical to the achievement of the 3-point increase in market share.

From a program perspective, the first two behaviors require information, and the second two behaviors require motivation and/or incentive. Even if they didn't know how to present the MSA or clinical reprint, reps might be motivated to try. But, there's only one thing worse than not presenting a message, and that's presenting a message poorly. So, when it comes down to it, all four changes in behavior are absolutely necessary.

"If you build it, he will come." That's a simple Core Message. But it only refers to one behavior, right? Wrong. It actually implies several other behaviors, including knowing how to build a baseball field, committing to the dollars required, being willing and able to plow over some of your cornfield, and a willingness to engage in regular ballfield maintenance!

The same goes for our friends at GlucaWell. Their ultimate outcome requires underlying knowledge and competency to deliver the critical messages, as well as the commitment to deliver them to the right people the right number of times. This is pretty typical. The behavior requires competency. In many cases, the competency has to be taught, learned and practiced. Launching a new product or a new sales tool or a new campaign or a new plan requires competency with the information.

THE OUTCOME MODEL™ ETERNAL TRUTH
Commitment to gaining the knowledge necessary to achieving the desired outcome is prerequisite to the successful application of The Outcome Model.™

Achieving this competency is part and parcel of changing audience behavior. It will be necessary for audience members to become proficient with the information before they can take on behavior-change-number-two, which is to present the information to the desired number of targeted physicians. If you don't have this in your audience, you need to get a new audience.

For this reason, "learn the material" may not be an expressed part of the core message. It may be implicit. If we say that presenting the information to our targeted physicians will result in increased market share, it is implied that we must present the information correctly. Correct delivery of the information, therefore, should be covered in the content of the program, and a way to test proficiency should be included as well.

Because the Core Message assumes competency in exhibiting the behavior, our key elements become:

- Share new MSA and/or Clinical Reprint (with proficiency) with 50% of target physicians by the end of the first quarter
- Personally deliver the Docs2Us.com information sheet and quick-sign-up authorization card to 100% of non-registered targets by

the end of the first quarter

It's important *not* to get caught up in all the possible iterations of a Core Message. Remember, Dr. Einstein, you want to be as simple and straightforward as you can be, without oversimplifying. That means making the direct connection between behavior and outcome. This isn't a crosword puzzle either. We're not asking the audience to put a lot of pieces together to determine the Core Message. Subtlety is our enemy here. So is over-complicating.

THE OUTCOME MODEL™ ETERNAL TRUTH
The Core Message filters all the "noise" surrounding a direct connection between behavior and outcome.

Start with this:

There's a lot of information here, and it could be argued that the core message is being lost in some of the numbers and timetables. The key to the connection between the change in behavior and the outcome is the action. The specifics of the numbers and timetables will be built into the content along with the information needed for proficiency. So let's put our filter on this model and see how it changes.

Filter out the noise and numbers, and the filtered version looks like this.

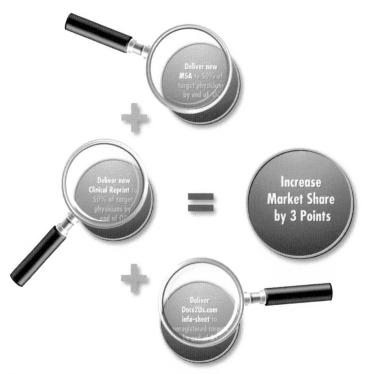

This filtered version is not intended to leave information out of the Core Message, but rather to concentrate on the elements of the message that are quickly understood and applied to the behavior itself. So the core message for our friends at GlucaWell is as follows:

All subsequent information in your program will now be built around this core message. Your content will show you what it means to present the new MSA correctly. Your training sessions will cover how the new Clinical Reprint is to be positioned, presented and talked about. Your call plans will include the presentation of the Docs2Us.com information and signup sheets, as well as the frequency and reach (number and targets) for each of these elements of the information to be presented.

A quick look back at our worksheets reveals that we have defined our desired outcome, identified the changes in audience behavior required to achieve the outcome, and built our Core Message around delivering on those changes. Look carefully to notice that each step is designed to deliver to the step before it. The Core Message delivers to the change in audience behavior, and the necessary changes in audience behavior we identified deliver directly to the desired outcome. This is exactly how the model should always work.

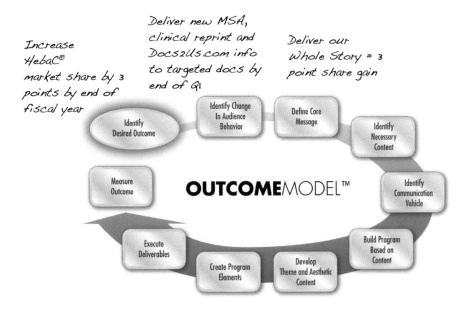

We've not only completed about 30% of our work. We have identified the key ingredients to achieving our desire outcomes, and we haven't even had to worry about delivering the information to our sales organization yet.

The great thing about The Outcome Model™ is that when you do finally get to the content part, identifying and building your content becomes simple. At this point, nobody should be "trying to decide what they're going to say" to the audience. The content will derive directly from the Core Message.

GREAT RAGWEED
Ambrosia trifida L.
RAGWEED FAMILY

CHAPTER SIX

Developing
the Necessary Content

"Sell it for more'n you got in it."

- A Contractor Friend

When I started in business many years ago, I asked a good friend of mine, Chris, who's a residential builder, if he would spend some time with me talking about good business habits. I figured, if you can make money building spec houses, you've probably got some good disciplines in place and some processes that might be applied to any business to make it more profitable, and if he didn't mind sharing it with me, I'd spend as long as it took to learn it.[20]

I was serious enough about this, that I told him I would buy him all the beer he could drink and dinner at one of our favorite restaurants. So, we met at an Athens institution called Allen's.

It's really a reconstitution, now, since the original owner and the guy who bought it from him have both died; the landlord ended up razing the old, dirty, dark and sketchy Allen's, to make room for a "mixed use" development (which has never materialized), and now Allen's is in a "new location" and "under new management" in a fine new building over on Hawthorne Avenue.

Families with little children come in now, and you don't see the old men

---

[20] This is an apocryphal story, much embellished for your pleasure. I think the real conversation took about a minute and a half, but you– the reading public– deserve better than that. So I'm making some of it up!

who used to beg the owner Danny for a beer at six a.m., when he really wasn't supposed to sell them one until much later in the morning, on the cusp of noon. He sold them anyway; sometimes he just gave them away, his heart being in the right place.

The burgers at the new Allen's taste just as good, but the fried hot dogs are no more; they've got a big beef dog they charge $4.95 for, and I just can't see paying that for a hot dog with no pork parts in it.

Anyway, in the interest of accuracy, this was a long time ago, and we were meeting at the old Allen's. After all, this was business.

Even though we were going to knock back a few cold ones and suck down a few fried hot dogs, I brought my note pad and even a little hand-held recorder, because it was my goal to absorb as much information as he was willing to give out. My friend's father had started the business many years before, and he'd bought him out recently, so there was all kinds of acumen and experience just waiting for me to tap into.

Being good southerners, we talked about family (mama 'n 'em, etc.) for about four beers prior to "ordering," which consists of yelling back over the counter the number of fried hot dogs you wanted and if you wanted onions on the side. Then we talked about his latest trip out west to shoot "bar" (really, he hunts bear...jeez).Then we got down to business. I pulled out my notebook and little recorder.

"What you doin'?" my friend asked me.

"Taking notes," I said.

"I thought you was smart," he said.

"I think I am," I replied.

"Not if you have to take notes," he said.

I put the pad away. I told him I didn't really even know where to begin when it came to running a business, but I thought I could learn and I was anxious to learn from him. I made him assure me that if I couldn't get all of the content in one sitting he'd let me buy him more beer at a later date to pick up where we had left off.

His chair creaked ominously as he leaned back in it and took a swig from his Budweiser.[21] He set the bottle down on the table.

"Well?" I said.

"Well, what?" he asked.

"What are your secrets to successful business."

He landed his chair back on four legs as he pointed to the waitress for another beer and looked at me intently.

"Whatever you sell…" he began.

"Yes?"

"Sell it for mor'n you got in it."

That was it. The sum total of his content for our mini-business-seminar. The girl delivered the hot dogs and his fifth beer, and that was it. Simple. To the point. But, probably a little shy of comprehensive. But it certainly gave me a place to start.

What I realized, of course, is that "Sell it for mor'n you got in it" is another great example of a core message. The content development stage

---

[21] What, do you think I'm cheap? I bought him the most expensive beer in the joint. I don't go to places with beer menus. I only go to places where, if you ask the waitress what kind of beer they have, she points to the taps at the bar, where you'll find, Bud, Bud Light and an occasional Miller High Life. I also don't eat at anyplace that calls itself an "eatery" any more than I'd go to a barber who called himself a "cuttery." And while we're on the subject, I'm not going in a store that's either "Ye Olde" or a "Shoppe." It's just how I roll…

begins after understanding that a successful business is built on selling whatever you sell... for mor'n you got in it. Armed with this succinct message, the real work of developing necessary content began.

THE OUTCOME MODEL™ ETERNAL TRUTH
Content has three jobs: to inform, to motivate, and to manipulate.

Inform, motivate, manipulate. It's pretty much what we do whenever we communicate with anybody. The first two appear very honorable and upstanding. And their definitions are pretty clear as it relates to The Outcome Model™.

Inform: Provide your audience with the knowledge required to achieve desired changes by teaching, training, and explaining.

Motivate: Instill in your audience the desire to make these changes by mapping the connection between action and result and by providing incentives for achieving the result.

The third job for content, as my physician often says when reading my blood pressure, "don't look so good." In fact, the third is pretty much the concept behind every "Lifetime Original Movie" that has ever aired. But don't be afraid of manipulation! We're going to bring this concept back into polite society right now. Not a single poisoning or burning bed will be experienced!

There's a much more benign definition of the word "manipulate" than the one used by Dr. Phil. And it's what we mean when we talk about the three jobs for cntent.

manipulate\mə-ní-pyə-lāt *v* : to manage or use skillfully.

See, if you're a manager, it's what you do every day! If you're a mom, it's what you do every day! If you run a baseball team or sell hot dogs at the ballpark, it's what you do every single day! Stand up for manipulation! It is a legitimate activity!

In fact, it's only way down the definition list that you begin to get into deceiving people for your own purposes and all that stuff, which is the polar opposite of effective content development. The whole point of developing effective content is to *tell the truth* about how particular actions will lead to a chosen outcome.

In the Outcome Model™, manipulation is about creating a pathway to an outcome by enjoining your audience to behave in a certain way. That's the difference between motivation and manipulation. Information provides the destination and road map. Motivation gives the reason to go; manipulation gives the kick in the pants. It is a demand we make of them, and it's not subtle. It may be palatable and reasonable, but it's not presented as a choice. It is artfully presented as an imperative.

Inform. Motivate. Manipulate. All three of these jobs must be done. Content isn't an either/or proposition. You have to have it all for any communication to yield results.

A Simple Prescription.
Did you ever hear that old adage about effective presenting? *Tell 'em*

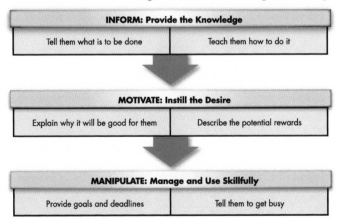

INFORM: Provide the Knowledge	
Tell them what is to be done	Teach them how to do it

MOTIVATE: Instill the Desire	
Explain why it will be good for them	Describe the potential rewards

MANIPULATE: Manage and Use Skillfully	
Provide goals and deadlines	Tell them to get busy

what you're gonna tell 'em. Tell 'em. Tell 'em what you told 'em.

I really hate that old adage. First, it's boring. Second, it's not true. My version of effective content development, while still simple, actually achieves the desired outcome.

This is the simplest prescription in the world for developing effective content that will support the core message, drive necessary changes in audience behavior, and achieve the ultimate desired outcome.

The art, of course, is in knowing the proper dosage and delivery of each element of the prescription. How much of each and how it's deliveredis different with every project or program. You may look at a commercial spot and see that it's heavy on the motivation. You might read a product brochure and find it focused almost entirely on the "How-to."A CEO's web-conference might be all about communicating corporate goals for the upcoming year, without going into operational details. The dosage and medicine will depend on what the audience needs to hear in order for them to do what you want them to do.

The delivery method will also depend on what the audience needs. Some people can take a big old horse pill. Others need a gel-cap. Some require spoon feeding, while others don't even flinch at the fattest hypodermic needle. We'll talk more about the delivery vehicle in the next chapter, but in the content development stages, you must understand your audience before you can understand what information is relevant to them.

You might even find that the natural progression of information-to-motivation-to-manipulation isn't necessarily effective in that order for a particular audience. It's quite possible that your audience wants to know the "what's in it for me" even before you deliver the goal. Here's an example.

Never listen to the side-effects. They'll make you sick!
Take a look at some of the direct-to-consumer drug advertising we've been seeing on television lately. For the most part, all of these commercials begin with "what's in it for me," which is the motivation part of the equation; they then move directly to the manipulation segment, with a direct call to action; finally they offer certain amount of information most of which is said very quickly and uses phrases like "sexual side effects."

There's one about an allergy medicine that works against allergies caused by things both inside and outside your house. It starts with a young woman talking about her issues with cats and dogs and flowers and pollen. Apparently the woman wasn't happy or comfortable anywhere (I bet she was a joy to be around!) until she found this medication which lets her breathe easy both indoors and out.

The magic of television allows her "haze" to be cleared up as she walks magically through a glass door (no cuts, broken glass or anything!), and right out there into the wild allergen-filled hell of a country meadow where despite all the ragweed, oak pollen, and dandelions, she's just smiling and breathing up a storm.

She instructs me to "ask my doctor" about this particular drug, and as she's headed toward a bunch of grazing sheep or something, a guy comes on and tells me all the horrible side effects I should look out for, not the least of which are two which reference "dizziness" and "death."Finally, they repeat that "Drug X is not for everyone. Ask your doctor."

Let us examine this spot. It essentially motivates, manipulates and then informs, in varying degrees of focus and importance.

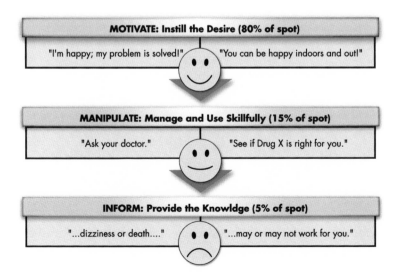

What is does NOT do is deceive. This commercial spot, for all its silliness, discloses the potential benefits and risks of this product, and it leaves it up to you to contact your doctor for her opinion. What is DOES do is focus on the most effective way of communicating benefits in a way that will motivate and manipulate a viewer to consider the benefits and take the desired actions, which is to ask his or her doctor.

THE OUTCOME MODEL™ ETERNAL TRUTH
Content must be designed around the truth and must never deceive in any way.

It's probably fair to say that most content focused on customers begins with motivation, while the majority of internal corporate content begins with information. This is only a general rule, however, as most sales representatives are very familiar with incentive programs whose announcements feature destinations and prizes long before they give the skinny on any specific goals, sales targets, or rules.

But generally, if you're telling it, you start with information; if you're selling it, you start with motivation.

Identifying necessary content.
Wherever we start, we need to be reminded of our core message, which connects the behavior changes we are advocating to the outcome we desire. They were all about delivering:

Our content should provide the information, motivation, and manipulation to make these behavior changes possible.

Let's start by going back to our initial worksheets to begin the process of developing the content we'll need for the program.

We'll find that a lot of the program content was written on those sheets as initial ideas for "desired outcomes." See, our hard work was worth while all along! So let's take a look at that first worksheet to see if we can quickly identify some of these content elements.

Understand marketing programs.

Execute processes.

Get more access to docs.

Understand the promotional materials.

Execute each sales call properly

Change docs prescribing habits.

Increase Market Share for Product A by 3 points

Get buy in on Docs2Us.com

On time! Under budget!

No off-label promotion!!!!

Follow the sales plan

~~Broad collaboration among teams with synergies~~

Represent our company the way you should

Use the Master Sales Aid!

One of the best ways to begin to identify content for whatever your program or communication vehicle is going to be is to add the words "How To" or "Why" to each of your initial entries. By doing so, you've actually drawn a content "skeleton" on which the flesh may be applied.[22]

---

[22] Let us very quickly clear up the difference between "flesh-out" and "flush-out." I do this as a public service for those of us who can't stand people mixing them up. Whereas you "flush out" a wound in order to remove germs, pus, poison, venom, broken glass, wooden stakes, bullet fragments, and so forth, you "FLESH out" an idea, as in adding flesh to a skeleton. To suggest that you want to "flush out" your CEO's idea is a poor career move at best. Please don't make me repeat myself on this.

As you do this, you'll begin to discover what content is critical to the support of the behavior change. You'll also begin to discover which elements of your content are needed to inform, motivate and move your audience to action.

Chart A

How to Understand marketing programs.

How to Execute processes.

How to Get more access to docs.

How to Understand the promotional materials.

How to Execute each sales call properly

How to Change docs prescribing habits.

How to Increase Market Share for Product A by 3 points

How to Get buy in on Docs2Us.com

How to (be) On Time! Under budget!

How to (avoid) No off-label promotion!!!!

How to Follow the sales plan

~~Broad collaboration among teams with synergies~~

How to Represent our company the way you should

How to Use the Master Sales Aid!

Chart B

How to Understand marketing programs.

~~How to Execute processes.~~

How to Deliver the New Clinical Reprint

~~How to Understand the promotional materials.~~

How to Execute each sales call properly

~~How to Change docs prescribing habits.~~

~~How to Increase Market Share for Product A by 3 points~~

How to Get buy in on Docs2Us.com

~~How to (be) On Time! Under budget!~~

~~How to (avoid) No off-label promotion!!!!~~

How to Follow the sales plan

~~Broad collaboration among teams with synergies~~

~~How to Represent our company the way you should~~

How to Use the Master Sales Aid!

On Chart A, we've added the words "How To," and we find that we have a great start on developing the necessary content. On Chart B we've eliminated redundant or overly general concepts or content that comprises a subset of others content. Here's why we crossed-out what we did.

- *How to execute processes* is very general and as such can't be measured. There are specific processes associated with some of the other elements, and those processes will be covered under content specific to those elements.

- *How to understand the promotional materials* will be covered under content specific to those promotional materials, such as the Master Sales Aid.

- *How to change docs' prescribing habits* is very important, and I know you think I'm making a mistake by removing it. But the fact is, changing these habits is really another way of saying "grow share." This makes it redundant. In addition, we believe that the new clinical information presented in both the Clinical Reprint and the new Master Sales Aid will provide the impetus for this change in habits.

- *How to be on time and under budget* isn't relevant to the desired outcome, which is to grow HebaC® market share by 3 points.

- *How to avoid off-label promotion* is important, but it should be well covered by any content covering the presentation of clinical data. Also, the best way to avoid off-label promotion is "not to do it." Not a contributor to the desired outcome.

- *Broad collaboration among teams with synergies* is still out. And, no matter how many times we type it, it still doesn't mean anything.

- *How to represent our company the way you should* is broad and can't be measured. It also something that is specifically addressed in each of the remaining elements. We're assuming that, if our audience learns to do the things that are left, they'll know how to represent our company the way they should.

Notice that we've also eliminated "Increase Market Share for HebaC®
by 3 Points," because it was elevated to the esteemed position of Desired Outcome. All content will be based on doing what is necessary to
achieve that outcome.

You'll also notice that we've re-named one! We believe that the new
clinical study about HebaC® will provide more than ample reason for a
physician to give us access. We know from the studies and from our
own anecdotal research that a doctor is most likely to see us when we
have new indications for our product or new clinical information. So,
we have replaced "how to gain more access" with "how to deliver the
new clinical reprint." Here's what's left.

Understanding Our Marketing programs

How to Deliver the New Clinical Reprint

How to Present the Master Sales Aid

How to Get buy in on Docs2Us.com

How to Follow the sales plan

How to execute each sales call properly

How vs. Why

You'll notice that we've moved each content topic to its own piece of paper, because it's now time to fill in the content details. Not surprisingly, each of these elements is what most management-types would call "tactical." And they'd be right. We've outlined what we need to do to INFORM them by identifying what needs to be done and the content that must be delivered to teach them how to do it.

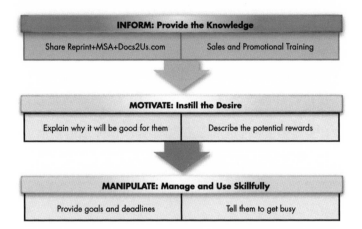

Our next step will be to MOTIVATE, or instill the desire to accomplish what we are telling and teaching them to do. Clearly this is a delicate balance between corporate motivators and personal motivators. In other words, we have to balance the corporate interest and self-interest to create a context in which both corporate and personal needs are met.

THE OUTCOME MODEL™ ETERNAL TRUTH
A successful motivator speaks to both the corporate and self-interest.

The reason is simple. Most people are driven both by self-interest and altruism. The majority of functional individuals you meet are generally trying to walk that line between their own self-interest and a broader community interest. It's why Dickens' *A Christmas Carol* continues to be a favorite during the holidays. It's why people weep at *It's a Wonderful Life*. People want to believe that the corporate interest—the community interest—wins in the end.

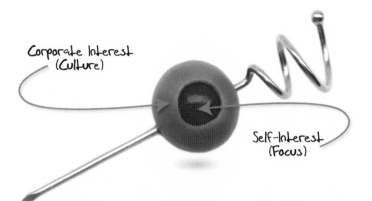

Corporate Interest (Culture)

Self-Interest (Focus)

But, let's put this balancing act into the proper perspective. For the most part, the corporate interest creates the culture or milieu, while the self-interest is a daily activity. If you asked a guy what kind of year he had, he's not usually going to tell you about his company's pursuit of its vision. He's going to talk about what he achieved personally. Corporate interest remains in the periphery, but the true focus is on the self-interest.

This is not a bad thing. Self-interest provides the catalyst for any incentive-based program, whether it is a compensation plan or some kind of annual contest. It's also this kind of self-interest that pushes just about any individual to the next level when it comes to improving performance.

To instill desire in an audience (or audience member) you have to create content that communicates both corporate and individual motivators. It's complex and heavily nuanced, depending on the audience or the organization, and it requires a full understanding of what makes your audience tick. The "dosage," if you will, depends on what you have to offer in the way of incentive compensation to reward the desired behavior.

Here's a fun little way to wrap your mind around it. Let's say you're watching a television commercial. If you hear a choir singing "We are the World" in the background, chances are the commercial is speaking to your altruistic nature and focusing on your relationship to a corporate or community interest. Now let's watch another commercial. Pink Floyd's singing "Money"; it's a safe bet they're trying to appeal to your self-interest.

Our friends at GlucaWell understand that they have created a culture stressing commitment to leadership in their therapeutic area, which means getting the effective product to more patients. This is a corporate/community motivator, because it means the audience and individual audience members have the ability to change and improve patients' lives.

The added benefit of committing to doing what is asked of them and assimilating the knowledge to that end is an increase in the number of prescriptions written by their target doctors. This is both a corporate and individual motivator, because their bonus plans are based on prescription goals. The company wins, and the individual wins.

The more specific the motivational content, the better. Target audiences appreciate targeted and specific messages that are easy to understand and assimilate. There's no point beating around the bush. Those guys putting out the television spot about the sinus medicine didn't. They sent that lady right out through her patio door into a world filled with the sights and scents of Ragweed City in the middle of Spring... and not a sneeze was to be had! She wanted to hang out with her ratty schnauzer dog in a field full of blowing dandelions and mewling feral cats, and by god, that's what she got! What could be simpler?

If you complicate the motivational message, you remove it from the emotional realm to the intellectual/critical realm. No good can come of this. Motivation is not an intellectual exercise. It's like running. At some point, it's not about technique. It's about the jogger's high. Motivation is when the endorphins kick in. A properly motivated target will go the distance.

One final thing about motivation. You had better not motivate with false promises. It takes about one split second to lose credibility with your target audience, and there's no antidote to that poison. Whatever you promise, you'd better follow through. This means being careful up front to develop motivational messages that are clear, concise and, above all, true.

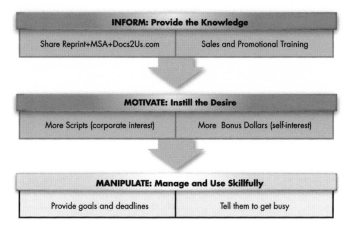

Specific good. General bad.

Some guys will tell you not to make specific promises. I disagree with that. A specific promise can be measured against reality and follow-through. A general promise will be *interpreted* by your audience, and they will often interpret in ways you didn't anticipate. Say you promise to take your audience "somewhere wonderful" if they achieve a certain sales goal by the end of the year. Nothing (and I mean *nothing*) good can come of this![23]

"Someplace Wonderful!"

---

[23] I think Chuck E. Cheese's is wonderful. Talk about ROI; years ago, after our kid's birthday party there, we actually came home with more children than we took.

While the lady in the picture was imagining a Hawaiian resort hotel, the boss was really thinking more of a "day trip" to a "fun" venue. This is a simple, yet significant, misunderstanding with far-reaching consequences.

Motivational content has to provide very specific information about actual and specific rewards for actual and specific behavior. Your audience needs to understand exactly what they will get by doing what you are asking them to do. In the allergy commercial, the reward was relief. The pharmaceutical sales organization, if they learn their stuff and execute it, will receive their full bonus. In both cases, the reward is very specific and straightforward.

> **"It is not the ship so much as the skillful**
> **sailing that assures the prosperous voyage."**
> -George William Curtis

George William Curtis, writer and political editor of *Harper's Weekly* in the 1860's had a good point about how the ship is steered. The same goes for manipulating an audience. Remember, the definition of the word "manipulate" is to ***manage or use skillfully***. This means to take the available resources and manage and use them to the desired end.

Thanks to our friends at the Online Etymology Dictionary,[24] we know that the word manipulate comes from the French word *manipule*, "handful," which was a pharmacist's measure (*manipule* deriving from the Latin *manus* for "hand" and the root of *plere* "to fill"). According to etymoline.com, the "sense of 'skillful handling of objects' is first recorded 1826" and extended shortly thereafter to the "handling of persons" as well.

This image of the pharmacist carefully measuring a drug applies beautifully to our understanding of building the content of our communications around the right measures of information and motivation... all

---

[24] This is a really cool resource that will take any word and help you understand its roots, where it came from, and how it came to mean what it does now. It will make you smarter and much better at "Jeopardy." Give it a try: **www.etymonline.com**. You won't be disappointed.

directed toward the desired end of reaching a measurable outcome. he proper "fill" of knowledge, motivation, training, and practice (in the case of our pharmaceutical company) equals changed behavior and successfully achieved outcomes.

Imagine driving down a highway. "Managing skillfully" requires the ability to make necessary adjustments along the way. If you imagine yourself driving a car down a highway, you'll notice that there's not a single moment when you are not making at least tiny adjustments to your direction, even on the straightest stretches.

You're adjusting the steering wheel in miniscule movements which reflect a knowledge of the changing landscape, road conditions, other drivers' actions, wind direction and speed changes, and any number of other changes to the environment which might take your car slightly off course.

This is not an involuntary process! It is a complex combination of sensory reactions, intuitive thinking, educated projection, hand-eye coordination, and focused decision-making. It is constant, requiring attention and knowledge- and experienced-based adjustments that are absolutely critical to the safe operation of the automobile. If you wonder why using a mobile phone is dangerous, think beyond the potential for running a red light or not seeing a bicyclist to the more subtle observations required to keeping a car on the road.

Failure to make such adjustments of less than 1/100 of an inch at a time will result in a head-on collision with that tractor-trailer truck less than 100 yards down the highway.

The best presenters do this when they're speaking to a group, selling to a single individual, following a business plan or managing a sales organization. They are keenly aware of environmental changes that will affect their outcome, and they have the knowledge and experience to make necessary adjustments. That's the skillful sailing Mr. Curtis was talking about.

Constant measurement of content effectiveness.
Our pharmaceutical executives have highlighted their goals and timelines, and they also have a way to measure progress. Their Sales Force Automation (SFA) program is a part of their overall Customer Relationship Management (CRM) model, and it provides a real-time snapshot of how each sales representative is doing against his or her goals.

By having this tool at hand, our impact isn't limited to the initial communication; the manipulation of the sales resource continues long after the lessons are taught and incentives are presented.

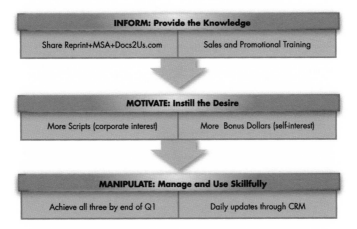

Of course, there's no room in a book like this one to "flesh out"our pharmaceutical company's content. What we can understand is the topics, and we can recognize the rationale behind the information they will present to support their core message. The content is very product - and - program-specific and probably wouldn't be too instructive here. But we can recognize that the challenges faced by our good friends at GlucaWell Pharma, Inc. are very similar to yours or mine. And we've now taken giant strides toward achievement of their desired outcome.

We've done the hard part. Now, for the next few chapters, we'll take on the fun part: executing an effective communications program that will deliver our desired outcome!

CHAPTER SEVEN

Choosing A Communication Vehicle

"If you do not change direction, you may end up where you are heading."

- Lao Tzu

T he truth about assumptions.

About twenty years ago, a large religious convention chose Atlanta for the site of its annual meeting and convocation. The flavor of the group was decidedly southern, and its members were well known for their fondness for soul food.[25] Any passionate endeavor requires ample fuel, and the assumption was that this group would require heaping helpings of fried chicken, mashed potatoes, collard greens, fried okra, black-eyed peas, biscuits and peach cobbler.

Proving that there's nothing more dangerous that a transplanted Yankee hotel executive come south with a superior attitude and time on his hands, one of the major downtown hotels decided that their "manna

---

[25] "Soul Food" refers to a style of cooking that originated with the African-American slave community primarily in the southern United States and has come to be associated with old-fashioned southern cooking. It is said to have derived from the creative preparation of the least desirable ingredients, cuts of meats, vegetables and so forth, but it now enjoys gourmet status among renowned chefs who have attempted to take fried chicken, collard greens, black-eyed peas and the like to new levels. They have failed. The best soul food will be found in "your mama's kitchen" or somebody else's mama's restaurant. Period.

from heaven" would arrive in the form of voracious Christians looking for fried food. And this hotelier was going to be ready come harvest-time.

I actually saw the Food and Beverage Director the day before the group arrived, and I swear he looked like Donald Duck when he's about to do evil to his nephews, all red-faced and with horns coming out of his head, and he was talking about how he was going to turn this big group of re-ligio-food zealots into the best month the hotel F&B department had had in years.

When I asked him how, he pointed to a long line of bare tables already set up in the middle of the atrium lobby, pre-positioned for the groaning weight of the largest soul food buffet in the history of downtown Atlanta, Georgia, way back to when it was called Marthasville and including the years immediately before and after Sherman' march. It was going to open at nine in the morning so attendees could take lunch to the hall with them, and it wouldn't close down until after midnight, long after even the most obsessed late-night snack-sneaker had gone to bed dreaming of biscuits and gravy.

He'd commandeered no fewer than three of the hotel's banquet kitchens and had them "ramped-up" for five straight days of heavy frying.

As the group checked in the following afternoon, their comments on the aroma of good things cooking was music to his ears. He implored his banquet staff to step up the pace, knowing that the throngs return-ing from their first service that evening would be famished and more than ready to pay twelve dollars for his fat-backed tribute to mamas everywhere.

He bustled up from his little office to the lobby around eight that evening as the first of the group returned from their praise service. Un-daunted when the first several clusters of well-dressed choristers passed the buffet without a sniff, his anxiety began to grow as group after group hurried along without stopping. His servers in their white aprons stood

up straight—their tongs, spoons, ladles and pie servers at the ready—
unmolested.

Fearing the group had scheduled a dinner at the convention center that
he hadn't known about, the Food and Beverage Director stopped one of
the older ladies to point out the buffet and ask why she hadn't stopped.

"Oh, it's a tradition, baby," she replied. "We *fast* for the week."

I don't know where this Food and Beverage Director works now, but I
think it's safe to bet that he does a little more investigating before he
starts heating up the Crisco. And so should you. Choosing a communications vehicle that will deliver your outcome is a lot like planning a
dinner for a group: they had better want to eat, and whatever you're
serving most assuredly will have to be to their liking. But one-out-of-
two won't get the job done.

Choosing with care.
Granted, sometimes you don't have a choice. You know that you're
going to produce a meeting for your sales organization, because through
careful assessment, this has proven to be the best way to communicate
new ideas, deliver new products, and train for new programs. In that
case, you will use The Outcome Model™ to determine the shape and
content of that program and execute to the outcomes just as you would
if you had come to the conclusion on your own that the meeting was the
right vehicle.

However, producing a meeting or any other communications vehicle
just because you've always done it that way isn't always the best idea
or the one that will deliver to your outcome. I once worked with an executive at a huge technology company who wanted to produce a road
show to sell his back-office hosting product to small- to medium-size
businesses. He had called on us because road-show development and
execution was one of our core services.

As we discussed his desired outcome, we determined that a thorough discussion of my client's product would require a time commitment on the part of a small business owner of between a half and a full day, without any assurance that the product was a viable solution to his challenges. We suggested that a small business owner, engaged in the daily operation of his or her business, might not be able to commit the time without a better understanding of the product beforehand.

We decided to ask.

THE OUTCOME MODEL™ ETERNAL TRUTH
The best way to gain insight is to ask a clear question and listen to the answer.

We employed a professional telephone interviewer to contact a sample of thirty-five owners and CEO's of small- to mid-size companies to find out how likely they would be to attend a road-show program and, if not, how they would like to receive information about this product offering if they were serious about exploring such a product.

Our goal here was not to reach any particular conclusion; it was to determine the best way to deliver our information to our target audience so that they would give it full consideration. We believed this full consideration was a critical step in the selling process. But, if we allowed them to talk us out of our original plan to hold a road show, we were placing a great deal of trust in our target audience. We had to believe that they, as business owners, would want to consider a product that would help improve and grow their businesses, and that they would tell us the truth about how best to present it.

Our research proved this to be the case. In almost every telephone interview, respondents suggested that they would like to have this information, and that if it was relevant to their businesses they would like to engage in an in-depth discussion with a representative of my client's company.

But they wanted to digest much of the information themselves before-hand. We decided to give ourselves over to this idea, even though we saw it as a risk. As it turned out, the prospects were telling us the truth. They did take time with the information when it was offered to them on their terms.[26]

Instead of producing a road show, we developed an interactive marketing tool (before interactive was cool!) which covered the essential value proposition of the product offering, along with product demonstrations, pricing models and client testimonials. Prospects were able to digest this information at their leisure, choosing the elements that were relevant to their businesses, and return to elements time and again for clarification.

The payoff was a higher number of prospects who were willing to meet with our client's representatives in person and discuss how the product offering would enhance their businesses specifically, when compared with a road show our client had produced the quarter before. The tool provided not only information that could be reinforced, but a method by which our client could continue to prospect without the larger investment of a road show.

Adding to its success, our program was produced for about the same budget as a single road show and could create opportunities for as long as the product offering remained the same. Revisions and enhancements to the module could be made as long as practical and financially sensible.

Here's the rub.
At the time, we didn't DO interactive marketing tools. Yikes. This could be trouble, unless you are willing and able to effect the kinds of changes

---

[26] This flew in the face of conventional wisdom that says the sales representative has to "own the pitch" from beginning to end. My first and best sales mentor, Bill Van Horne, taught me never to let a prospect hold the presentation book. He didn't want them leafing through it and making assumptions about what each page meant. I almost got in a fight with a prospect once who tried to wrestle my book away from me. I took him, though. He was in his sixties, and I was 23.

that might be necessary when you use The Outcome Model™.

Early in this book I said this: *"Outcome thinking may be counter-intuitive. It might burst bubbles or put cracks in the patina of accepted practice. It might show somebody that he or she is wrong."* This particular client proved it. And now we had to make adjustments to fulfill the responsibility that The Outcome Model™ had placed on us.

Not to take anything away from all the fine technicians who make a living writing, producing advertising spots, composing music, building sets, designing print pieces, planning meetings, or developing interactive marketing tools (after all, I'm one of them), but there are lots of great technicians out there, and once you've reached the point of choosing a communications vehicle, you're already assured of success. You've already served as your own great architect. Now, you just don't want to screw it up by hiring lousy builders.

And now that we were in the business of designing and producing an interactive marketing tool—whose inner workings we already understood, because we'd done the hard work to find out—we had plenty of partners to help us make it wonderful. It's really simple: how you communicate your content will be determined by the decisions you've made all along the Outcome Model™ path.

A national sales meeting.
Let's take a look at where our executive team at GlucaWellfinds itself.

- The team has identified the desired outcome, which is relevant, realistic and measurable
- They've outlined the key changes in behavior that will have to take place for this desired outcome to be realized
- The Core Message compels the audience to deliver the entire story about the company in order to gain share
- They've identified the content necessary to provide all the tools necessary for living up to the Core Message

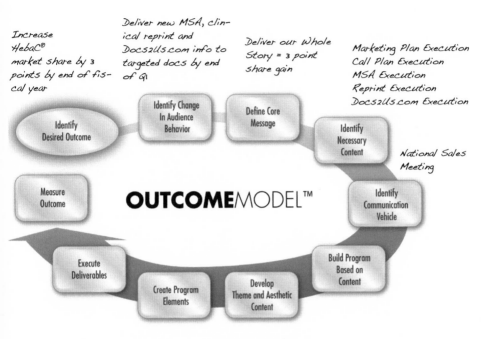

At this point, let's pay particular attention to the content that we've identified as necessary to the outcome. Let's remember that this content provides our audience with the tools they will need to fulfill the promise inherent in the Core Message. The promise they have made is to deliver the company's "whole story" represented in three key elements of the marketing program to achieve an expressed growth in market share.

The majority of this content is very specific, somewhat rote (as a lot of pharmaceutical selling is due to FDA regulations), and will require intense training, practice, and repetition.

By now, it doesn't take a brain surgeon to figure out that a lot of this stuff is based on a simple, logical, and rational approach to taking steps that make sense. "Of course," you might say, "everybody knows that!" And, it seems pretty obvious that a National Sales Meeting or some kind of company-wide training conference is necessary to deliver the kind of in-depth information necessary for sales representatives to deliver the company's "whole story."

DUH, you say. But what if...

Well, you can just hold that "pshaw" for a moment.[27] The reason this method of delivering our content is so obvious is that The Outcome Model™ works! It's a "big DUH" because it has been vetted through a rigorous process. It is the rigor and discipline of the process that leads so logically to each of the next steps.

<u>THE OUTCOME MODEL™ ETERNAL TRUTH</u>
Rigor and discipline in each stage of The Outcome Model™ make the subsequent stage easier and more obvious.

The answer may seem simple and obvious. But let's go back to the beginning for a minute and change just one variable. Suppose our Vice President of Marketing came from a sales background and was a little more forgiving of sales representatives "finding their way." It's possible that she would have been happy with their delivery of the Master Sales Aid as it was originally constructed and that her approach to Docs2Us might have been more casual. There might not be a big push for the sales organization to "understand the marketing program."

In that case, it's quite possible that the marketing focus would be purely on the new Clinical Reprint, which describes recent findings regarding the product's *efficacy*. In the end, the change in behavior might be limited to delivering the new reprint to 50% of targeted physicians by the end of the first quarter. Consequently, the core message might well be "Deliver the New Clinical Reprint to grow market share by 3 points."

Would you hold an entire national sales meeting just to teach the Clinical Reprint? Maybe not. It might be done in a simple video. It could be done on a regional basis with local physicians. It might even be a road show driven by trainers who travel to the districts. It might just be an annotated version of the reprint. See the difference?

---

[27] Actually the only person I ever knew who used that word was a classmate at Virginia named Mike Gladstone who became a very highly regarded attorney. Whether he has ever used the word "pshaw" on a jury is anyone's guess, but my money's on yes. And in case you have a regional bias against soul food and southern interjections, "pshaw" can actually be found in the dictionary, defined as "expressing disbelief, impatience, or contempt." The French have a word for it, too: "peuh!" Seriously. You can look it up!

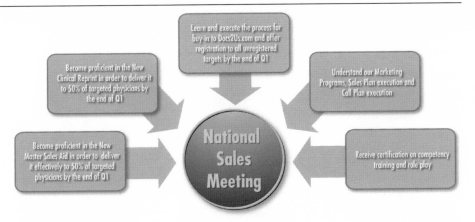

The broad content needed to drive successful application of our original Core Message will certainly require a national meeting.

Not so with only a single change in audience behavior. If our only change is to deliver the new Clinical Reprint materials proficiently, a lot of things are different, including The Core Message and the content driving it. Here, the quantity of content could be delivered in any number of ways and still be effective. This doesn't mean you wouldn't have a national meeting if there were other outcomes to be delivered, but the single new reprint, by itself, wouldn't warrant one.

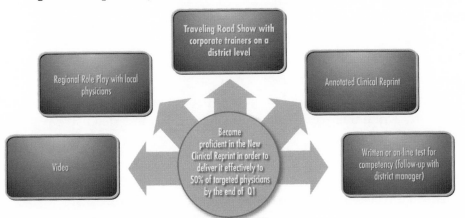

Outcome management of periodic challenges.
As we've discovered, The Outcome Model™ is media neutral. It doesn't care whether you deliver The Core Message via satellite, sky writing, or smoke signal, as long as the total focus is on the outcome and attendant behavior changes necessary to achieve it. The advantage here is

that The Outcome Model™ allows smart people to make adjustments to their approach when periodic challenges present themselves. Because your message and content are tightly focused on the outcome, you can change the way you actually present your content and still realize the desired outcome.

We recently helped a client save upwards of a million dollars by replacing his national sales meeting with a "virtual meeting." You'll find that people have a wide range of definitions of virtual meetings, ranging from "webinars" to satellite broadcast of management presentations, but our Outcome Model™ exercise told us that this sales organization needed a lot more than talking heads to help them succeed in a challenging market.

Because this highly-regarded company with its super-recognizable brand is tied to the construction and remodeling industries, their field sales force has found it a challenge to continue to meet high growth expectations. Granted, everybody is under this same gun, but this company is unwilling to partici-

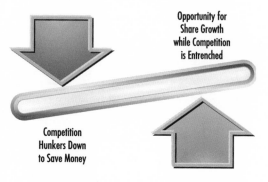

Opportunity for Share Growth while Competition is Entrenched

Competition Hunkers Down to Save Money

pate in the contraction, and their goal is to grow market share in a down economy while their competitors are entrenched in a defensive position.

At the same time, a million bucks is a million bucks, and senior management directed our client to cut the budget and still grow share, thank you very much. What's wonderful about The Outcome Model™ is that it rises to such challenges!

Because in preparation for their annual national sales meeting we had worked with our client through The Outcome Model™, we had already identified their desired outcome, necessary changes in audience behavior, core messaging and content. It was as we were moving to the execution stages that we received word that the program in its current form was being cancelled.

Yikes again. But we didn't have to start over! All we had to do was identify what delivery methods were available to us, given the technology and cost, and then see if and where we might have to compromise on content.

THE OUTCOME MODEL™ ETERNAL TRUTH
Periodic changes in circumstances that do not affect the outcome should not take the focus from the outcome.

Our outcome never changed. This particular client, like our friends at GlucaWell, had a particular share growth goal, and we believed that we could still achieve this growth in a challenging economy and with a different kind of communications vehicle.

We didn't want to be driven by technology.
It will be my pleasure to discuss later the evils of technology leading outcome around by the nose. I believe that the master is the desired outcome, and the technology should serve "at the pleasure" of the master[28].

So when our attention turned to some kind of web stream (since, for the amount of content a satellite broadcast was out of the question financially), we quickly dismissed it. Not that a streaming webcast isn't cool; it is, in a kind of "e-trade baby" sort of way. But streaming video over

---

[28] This, of course, coming from a man whose dog puts her paw on his knee when she wants him to get off the couch so she can lie down. And he does it.

the web would not enable us to pay proper homage to one of the most important elements of the client's brand: the beauty of its product.

Our client's brand is built on the company's design and engineering sensibility. I've been fortunate enough to watch a photo-shoot for one of their products, and it is a thing of beauty. Only an inanimate object could suffer through such attention to perfection; it would kill a fashion model.

So we couldn't sacrifice the quality of the product images when it came to presenting new products and technologies. This was to become the key determining factor in the new communications vehicle we chose: **High Definition DVD**. It would allow us to produce a high-quality program, with high-definition images of both the product and the program elements, and it gave us an opportunity to add high-energy music, video, and entertainment elements at will.

Respecting the audience's time.

It also allowed us to do one other thing that we hadn't even thought of when we began the process. Using HD-DVD allowed us to present a program that could be viewed on the viewer's timetable (within reason) when he or she was most likely to give it full, uninterrupted attention.

The DVD (to be viewed in a prescribed sequence) featured senior management presentations, key goal-setting information, an overview of global initiatives, and sales "marching orders." In addition, viewers were treated to a series of "workshops," 15-minute presentations from the product marketing teams on product introductions and marketing programs. These workshops were scripted in a "morning show" format to keep them light and lively while still covering all of the critical information.

Ultimately, the package consisted of a targeted DVD (based on whether the sales associate's focus was on retail or wholesale customers), an in-depth binder of learning materials and product information, a variety of collateral materials to help reinforce the message and content, a narrated, self-playing PowerPoint presentation announcing and honoring award winners for the previous year, a package announcing and explaining an incentive contest, and various other elements specific to specific sales teams.

Each member of the sales organization was given 10 days to watch and study the materials, after which districts participated in conference calls with product and brand teams to discuss and ask questions. The decision to cancel the meeting was made the week of Thanksgiving; the "meeting in a box" was delivered to the sales organization in mid-February.

And, to top it all off, the presentation of the content received higher scores on the DVD than at either of the two previous meetings.

While the ultimate desired outcome, solid growth in market share for the year, hasn't been measured at this writing, the receptiveness of this particular audience to the message, combined with the comprehensive nature of the information and tools included in our "meeting in a box," should provide the audience with everything they need to achieve the desired outcome. And we're told the trends are positive.

Whether they choose to go back to meeting in person or not, and we have to presume they will, this particular client learned a valuable lesson about content. When all was said and done, the content we put together for an audience that would be viewing it on their own had to be more succinct, more self-explanatory, and clearly more thorough (even when presented in smaller chunks) than the traditional 90 minute "workshops" they had been producing at the national meeting. This told us something about the method and effectiveness of delivering content to this particular audience and will change the way we produce live workshops in the future.

But whether The Outcome Model™ proves our intuition right or wrong when it comes to how we deliver the content, we profit from knowing that any delivery method, to provide a true return on our investment, must deliver directly to the outcome.

CHAPTER EIGHT

Execution

"Mechanical excellence is the only vehicle of genius."

- William Blake

THE OUTCOME MODEL™ ETERNAL TRUTH
Execution begins with the mechanical delivery of the intellectual product of the outcome process.

This simple definition describes a final physical manifestation of an intellectual process. It's the "thing" we "thought up." But what I said in the chapter on discovering your Core Message is true for the execution of your chosen communications vehicle: the "big idea" isn't found in the execution itself; it is the purpose of the execution. The big idea is the outcome that the execution generates.

Most organizations are defined and judged by what they deliver. It doesn't matter whether you manufacture, landscape, paint portraits, oversee a church, or direct a sales organization that markets an important pharmaceutical. Your success and the value of your product is generally based on how people perceive what you "make" or the service you provide. The same goes for communicating a desire outcome.

If you think beyond the delivery of that shiny new product, you'll discover that customers' real impression of you and your product (and your "net worth") will ultimately be based not on what that product *is* at the moment of delivery, but what that product *does* for them later on down the line. It is, in essence, the *fruit* of your labor that they will judge, based on what it bears *for them*.

129

- Does your vacuum cleaner continue to perform well, and will all the bells and whistles you invented still have meaning for the consumer five years from now?

- Will the beautiful landscaping you install today continue to thrive in this environment in the years to come? Are those dogwoods set far enough apart to mature comfortably, and will the gardenia plants bloom twenty years from now as the trees cast more shade?

- Will the portrait you paint this year capture your subject as a young girl and allow people to recognize those same intelligent eyes in her when she becomes an old woman?

- Will the Thanksgiving dinner you provide for the needy people of your community become the seed for a sustainable feed-the-hungry effort for years to come?

- Will the meeting you produce for your sales organization result in a competent marketing effort and three point share growth?

These questions are audacious ones that assume we can actually have a sustainable impact on our audience or on the consumer of our products and services. That's to say the effect of our products live long after the initial transaction and long after the shine wears off.

This is the groundwork for successful execution of the communications vehicle. However you execute it, the vehicle must ultimately get the audience where it needs to go. You can put all kinds of "options" on it, but be careful that the options don't "interfere with the safe operation of the vehicle,"and that the vehicle continues to run long after the test drive.[29]

I often remind executives that they "serve at the pleasure of their audi-

---

[29] The automobile metaphor, while mildly irritating, is also timely, as Chrysler and General Motors declared bankruptcy while I was writing this book. While I don't pretend to be an industry expert, it's pretty safe to say that these companies' failures were due, at least in part, to not executing to a relevant, realistic, and measurable outcome.

ences." This means the only measure of what a speaker has to say is the benefit the audience receives. If you're not giving them something they can use for their benefit, don't bother flapping your gums. You shouldn't be up there.[30]

THE OUTCOME MODEL™ ETERNAL TRUTH
Every communication is a business-to-business transaction. It must result in a profit for each party.

Every single communication with customers, internal staff, partners, sales organizations, or even friends, is a business-to-business transaction and is judged as such. Every communication involves a measurable exchange of capital.

There's a guy who used to work for me who was always talking about "B2B and B2C". They're both quasi-acronyms that distinguish business-to-business transactions from those taking place between businesses and consumers. I, for one, don't believe there is any difference between the two, especially when it comes to communication. I believe *every* transaction is a business-to-business transaction and that every communication follows suit. There must be profit on both sides of the transaction in order for it to be a success.

Consumers measure profit in taste, healthfulness, economy, effect on lifestyle, financial growth, happiness, knowledge gained, and so forth. It is a profit/loss equation every time. Ask the guy who walked out of a lousy movie after spending forty bucks on tickets, popcorn, and watery soda what his P&L Statement looks like.

Every conversation has the potential for giving to or taking from a participant. People engage in conversations for all kinds of reasons, but rarely do people want to waste time if they don't get anything (fun,

---

[30] The same can be said of writing a book. And you will be the judge of whether I have served at your pleasure. If not, please let me know. Just don't send the book back; I have way to many of them piled up here as it is!

knowledge, enjoyment, bonding, friendship) out of it. How often do you beg your neighbors who just got back from their family vacation at Myrtle Beach to come over and spend an evening showing you pictures of the Wet n' Willie Water Park or Safari-Slice Mini-Golf? About never? That's what I thought.

My friend Sandy (another of my golf buddies, who would be more prominent in this book if any of his jokes were appropriate; none is) tells a story of his dad who discovered the internet at the age of 85. Sandy was over at his folks' house one evening and, as his mother relayed a long story about a distant cousin, his father worked feverishly on his new laptop computer.

"What are you looking up there, Dad?" Sandy asked.

"I'm Google-ing to see if there's a cure for incessant chatter," the old man said.

Execution should combine precision with performance.
Sounds kind of like a sports car, doesn't it? But in this case, precise handling and impressive horsepower are replaced with precise messaging and compelling delivery.

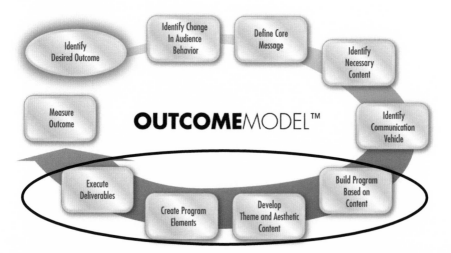

In The Outcome Model™ there are four elements of execution: building an effective program, developing a theme and/or aesthetic context, creating the essential program elements, and executing the deliverables. The order of these steps is very important, because like the other steps of the Outcome Model™, each step informs and provides the foundation for the subsequent step.

These four elements comprise what the audience will see, what they will feel, what benefits they will receive, and what they will do as a result. Execution is the successful delivery of every one of these steps.

But, what they see, feel, and judge pales in comparison to what they do as a result. The *successful* execution of a program can only be measured by whether it leads to the achievement of the desired outcome. My late dad was a communications executive at The Coca-Cola Company, and he used to tell me a soft drink spot might make you weep with joy, but "if it doesn't sell pop, it's not worth a damn."

I'm not saying "the end justifies the means."
This is not to imply that it doesn't matter how you execute, that as long as you achieve your desired outcome it's okay. Quite the contrary, how you execute will determine not only whether you achieve your outcome, but how effective and sustainable your core message will be to drive the outcome for the long haul.

It takes both show and business to achieve the desired outcome. This is where many communications professionals fall short of their charge; they spend so much time, energy and financial resources on the show, that they lose the business outcome. Everybody had a great time, but nobody did anything after the show. The operation was a total success, but, of course, the patient—the business outcome—died.

THE OUTCOME MODEL™ ETERNAL TRUTH
Execution can do a lot of things, but above all, it had better " sell pop".

And, the more you spend on execution, the more pop you'll need to sell to justify your investment. This is a simple equation that we'll cover in the chapter on measurement, but it's important enough to bring up in this section, too. When you look at budgeting for a particular level of execution, or when you begin to make choices about what elements are important or not, the ultimate measure of importance is what the element delivers to the outcome.

Let's consider the elements.

VEHICLE	FORM
Workshop	Curriculum
Video	Storyboard
Meeting	Agenda
Brochure	Layout
Tradeshow Exhibit	Traffic Plan
Speech	Outline
Interactive Module	Site Structure
Sales Pitch	Deck

Build program based on content

This is really an exercise in logic and in laying out the order and flow of elements that will best support the content and deliver the core message. It is here that you begin to choose how you want the content to be delivered to its fullest effect.

The flow comes in many different forms, depending on what vehicle you have chosen.

How you develop this flow may be very different depending on your choice of vehicle, and there's definitely an art to it. Some creative types might suggest that developing a storyboard for a television spot is the more artistic exercise when compared to building an agenda for a meeting or a curriculum for a workshop. That is vocation-centric arrogance and ought to be illegal![31] It doesn't matter what form this step takes; the

---

[31] Of course if creative arrogance were against the law, what would happen to all the tattoo parlors? Or the coffee houses? Or, for that matter, the goatee? Or micro-brews? Oh, the humanity.

purpose of it is the same, and the thinking process is identical. Ultimately, whatever you do, it had better "sell pop."

The Sales Pitch is a great way to envision how this process works, because you essentially have a stack of slides (content) that are put in the most effective order to achieve the ultimate outcome, which is making the sale. The deck is very flexible; you can move slides around and change information and design at will, so aside from the inclusion of essential content, you can do just about whatever you want to do, which is both a blessing and a curse. What do you do?

A sales pitch for the Outcome Model™

Let's suppose my desired outcome is to produce an Outcome Model™ workshop for a certain

 dollar amount that assures a healthy but reasonable profit. The workshop is already "in the can" and ready to go. I've got my pricing worked out, and I've got a prospect on the line. How do I proceed?

Well, if we follow The Outcome Model™ (which one should expect we would!) we know the following things:

DESIRED OUTCOME:	Profitable production of workshop
CHANGE IN AUDIENCE BEHAVIOR:	Consider merits Receive proposal Sell internally Sign contract Pay bill
CORE MESSAGE:	OM workshop will result in achievement of desired outcomes at your company
NECESSARY CONTENT:	Value of achieving outcomes Importance of outcome-focus Measurement as indicator of success Steps to completion Necessity of executive competency Proof of effectiveness of workshop Value equation
COMMUNICATIONS VEHICLE:	In-person sales presentation
BUILD PROGRAM BASED ON CONTENT:	Deck

We're clearly ready to execute the sales presentation. We know what we want our audience to do; we've identified our core message; we're clear on the content we need to present to inform, motivate and manipulate, and we've chosen our communications vehicle, which is an in-person sales presentation.

The deck isn't the presentation.
Now we have to build our program, which in this case is a deck. But let's be clear: the deck isn't the presentation. The deck provides a guideline for the presentation and plays a supporting role in making the presentation. It really is your "storyboard" for the pitch. It's certainly not dynamic enough to stand on its own the way a video or commercial spot might. The phrase "Death by PowerPoint" didn't come from a presenter; it came from a miserable audience member. But it is a valuable tool for organizing the program and flow, and it provides the foundation for the delivery of the aesthetic content and creation of the program elements themselves.

Spread out the content.
Of course, the content gives us the first clue to what goes in the program and in what order it is delivered. Those of you who do everything on computer might find it amazing that some of us actually still use index cards to organize our thoughts and flow. You might want to try this. Put each content heading on an index card and spread them out in front of you. This will give you a broad perspective on what you need to deliver, along with a flexible way to move things around. Let's try it:

outcome model steps	return on investment	case studies of other projects

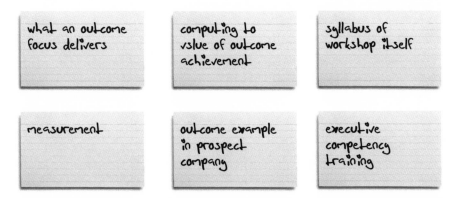

We know we have to deliver all of this information in order for the prospect to make a sound decision about investing in an Outcome Model™ workshop. At this point we haven't identified the order, the flow, the importance of each topic relative to the others, or the logical organization of the pitch. We've only taken the content and spread it out.

Categorize the content.
The next step is to categorize the content elements. This means associating similar content into a broader category. By doing so, you'll begin to see a pattern that you'll use to build a logical flow. For the time being, we've identified three catagories: product (p), case studies (c/s), and value (v).

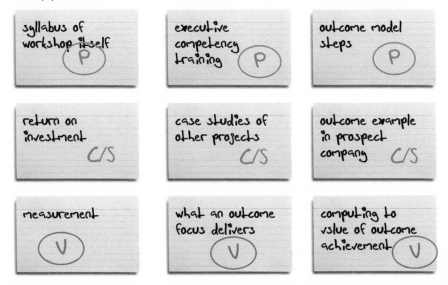

Organize the content.

After taking the corresponding content and clustering it, it's time to get a little "finer" with the flow, by thinking through what each element of content is intended to do, where and when it is best presented, and in what order it is most likely to compel the desired action.

The program blocks are nearly in place, and we can begin to see that our delivery, similar to that of our friends with the allergy medication earlier in the book, begins with motivation. We start by showing value; we follow up with detail; and then we close the deal with proof.

The program flow essentially ends up looking like this:

Section One: Value

Section Two: Product

Section Three: Proof

I won't go into the actual sales presentation with you, because one day I might be in your office, in front of you, giving you the same pitch! I wouldn't want to bore you... But once I've got the program itself figured out, it's now time to build an aesthetic context.

138

Developing a theme and aesthetic content.
Now that you've reached this point in The Outcome Model™ here's a shocker for you. Most people *START* with the theme!

"They start the execution phase with the theme?" you ask.

"No," I answer. "They start the *whole process* with the theme!"

"Say it ain't so," you intone.

But it is. I can't begin to tell you how many vice presidents of sales have told me that they want to have their meeting at a golf resort with the theme, "Playing to Win." When I ask what will be covered at the meeting, they often tell me "we haven't decided yet," or (more dangerously), "the usual."

Now, I must admit, I wish I had a boss who would take me to a golf resort for our national sales meeting, and I can assure you that I wouldn't complain about receiving "the usual," as long as it meant good food, a fancy resort, and free golf. But this kind of thinking almost always shortchanges the content because it drives the content to support the theme, rather than the other way around. Likely as not, the audience will end up listening to an expensive motivational speaker talk about how "Selling is Like Golf: Drive for Show and Putt for Dough."

You'll often find that these kinds of meetings are also focused on who is speaking rather than what they're saying. Here's how a typical planning meeting sounds:

"Okay, who's gonna present this year?"

"Well, we got to start with the CEO; he missed last year because of his divorce."

"What's his topic?"

"I think he made a work-life balance presentation to the board a couple weeks ago; maybe he could re-purpose that."

"Great. Who's gonna ask him?"

"I will."

"Okay."

"If we don't put H.R. up there we'll never her the end of it. She's kinda irritated with us anyway."

"All right. And Bob and I'll do our dog and pony show."

"Has Bob got anything new from marketing this year?"

"Not really, but we want to show the field how well we're collaborating."

"Point taken. That means we better put the service guy up there for a presentation. What's his name?"

Anyway, it goes on and on like this until they finally get to the very last presentation on the last day, which is unfailingly titled, "Marching Orders".

If you're all about outcomes, you know this to be true:

"Insanity is doing the same thing in the same way and expecting a different outcome."
- Chinese Proverb

Every project and every element of every project is different. They need to be given that kind of respect.

It's also easy to get caught up in the creative excitement of developing a theme for a meeting or a "big idea" for a commercial spot or video or whatever, but it's important to remember that the aesthetic content and theme are outcome-driven. Without this outcome-focus they are apt to take on a life of their own which tends to get expensive both in terms of money and people resources.

I knew of one company that always chose their theme before anything else, and they liked to build on it from one year to the next. They wanted to drive home the notion that they were a visionary company, and that they were always thinking "outside the box". Unfortunately, this left them in somewhat of a physics quandary after a handful of meetings.

YEAR ONE THEME: On the Road!
YEAR TWO THEME: On the Horizon!
YEAR THREE THEME: Beyond the Horizon!

Now I ask you. Just where were they supposed to go next? Toward the light? You'd think they would have foreseen the difficulty of sustaining a run that consistently placed their goal farther and farther away! After three years, I think they just settled on "Playing to Win."

The theme for a program has only two purposes:

1. To provide a memorable, shorthand version of the Core Message

2. To create a thematic context that ties other aesthetic content to the Core Message

These days, you have to justify nearly every expenditure with a definite return on investment, and the only way to do that is to come by your theme honestly. This means the theme and aesthetic content are a natural derivative of the outcome thought process. They have to do what every other element of the Outcome Model™ does; they have to deliver to the outcome.

THE OUTCOME MODEL™ ETERNAL TRUTH
Aesthetic content is only worth the investment when it makes the delivery of the content more effective.

Do you remember that insidious song "A Spoonful of Sugar"? It was written by the Sherman brothers (Robert and Richard) in 1964 for the movie *Mary Poppins*.[32] As repugnant as that song was, it pretty adequately describes the whole purpose of creating a theme or aesthetic context for a program or communications vehicle of any sort. It makes the content (which is good for you) easier to swallow and more interesting. It also makes the content and Core Message more memorable. And, it is absolutely a derivative of the outcome. It has to be.

Desired Outcome:	3 Point Market Share Gain
Change in Audience Behavior:	Present new Master Sales Aid to 50% of targeted docs by end of Q1 Deliver New Clinical reprint to 50% of targeted docs by end of Q1 Deliver Docs2Us.com information sheet and quick sign-up authorization card to 100% of non-registered docs by end of Q1
Core Message:	Deliver our whole story and we will achieve a 3 point share gain
Necessary Content:	Understanding our marketing strategy Perfecting Sales Plan execution Perfecting Call Plan execution Mastering the new MSA Mastering the new Clinical Reprint Steps to Docs2Us.com buy-in
Communications Vehicle:	National Sales Meeting
Build Program Based on Content:	Agenda

Let's take a look at GlucaWell Pharma again. They've done a lot of work so far; they know they're producing a national sales meeting for their group, and they know it's going to be full of really good content. Let's see how they arrive at a theme. Here's the box score of where they are now.

---

[32] My grandfather took me to see this awful film one Friday after school. When it was over, he told me I was old enough to start going James Bond films. I think it was because of *Mary Poppins* that I was 7 when I saw my first "Bond Girl."

Because this is a meeting, the flow of the program is expressed in an agenda, which outlines speaker presentations, workshops, team-building and social activities, meals, and so forth. This is essentially a three-day meeting, with attendees arriving the evening before, and an overview of the agenda looks something like this:

TRAVEL DAY		
Afternoon	REGISTRATION	
Evening	WELCOME RECEPTION	
DAY ONE		
7:30-8:45 am	BREAKFAST	
9:00-Noon	GENERAL SESSION	
9:00-9:30	Grow Share by 3 Points!	V.P. Sales
9:30-10:00	Marketing Plan Strategy	V.P. Marketing
10:00 -10:45	Master Sales Aid Overview	Product Manager
10:45-11:15	BREAK	
11:15-11:40	Clinical Reprint Overview	Medical Director
11:40-11:55	Docs2Us.com Overview	Dir. Sales Operations
12:00-1:00 pm	LUNCH	
1:00-5:00	WORKSHOPS (Rotating)	
2 Rotations	Master Sales Aid Training	Training Department
2 Rotations	Clinical Reprint Training	Training Department
6:00-8:00	RECEPTION/DINNER	
DAY TWO		
7:30-8:45 am	BREAKFAST	V.P. Sales
9:00-10:10	GENERAL SESSION	Dir. Sales Operations
9:00-9:30	Sales Execution	Regional Directors
9:30-9:50	Sales Plan Execution	
9:50-10:10	Call Plan Execution	District Managers
10:10-10:30	BREAK	
10:30-Noon	Call Plan Workshop	
	In District Meetings	Training Department
12:00-1:00 pm	LUNCH	
1:00-5:00	Role Plays	

What you see in this agenda is a flow of content that is absolutely true to the discoveries our executive team has made as they have worked their way through the Outcome Model™. The heavy emphasis in this meeting is on the three things the sales guys need to present to the physicians to change their prescribing habits. The message is: do these things, and we'll grow share by at least 3 points.

The theme, like many of the steps in the Outcome Model™ is writing itself. It's a three day meeting; there are three things that need to be done; the reward is three point share growth. It's a simple, yet powerful theme that says it all. Do these three things… gain these three points.

Three for Three!
It provides quick and memorable support to the Core Message, and there are all kinds of things that can now be done with this theme in terms of graphics, team building programs, speech and presentation content and so forth. The theme fulfills its purpose.

What's interesting about the simplicity of this theme is that it is a simple derivation of statements that our executive team made early on. This certainly helps validate our decision. Remember what they said?

VP of Marketing: "This is all about our competency with the marketing strategy."

Product Manager: "They need to present the Master Sales Aid and clinical reprint correctly for this to have any effect on their prescribing habits."

| VP of Sales: | "We have to grow share, and having something new to tell these physicians is the key." |

As my friend Chip Hill, our ace pitcher in high school used to say whenever he'd strike out the side: "Right on. Right on. Right on."

Creating program elements and executing deliverables.
If you're reading this book (and my guess is, you are,) you are no doubt highly educated in the method and process of executing programs. The Outcome Model™ is about arriving at the execution stage with the information you need to create and build a program to the end that the outcome is achieved.

What elements you choose and how you choose to execute them is a function of everything you've learned thus far. I could write an entire book on creating program elements and "executing to excellence." But we'll save that for another day.

What I will tell you is this. Don't stop using The Outcome Model™ when you get to the individual elements. Not only should each element dance to the tune of the desired outcome for the program; every element should be approached with its own Outcome Model™.

THE OUTCOME MODEL™ ETERNAL TRUTH
Every executable element should be produced using its own miniature Outcome Model™.

Let's go back to the agenda for the National Sales Meeting and take a look at the program elements. If we're true to The Outcome Model™ we've developed for the meeting, each individual piece of the program will play a role in the delivery of the Core Message, communication of the tools that are needed to change behavior, and final outcome. Here are the executable elements:

- Pre-Meeting Promotion
- Registration
- Welcome Reception
- Presentations:
  - Grow Share by 3 Points
  - Marketing Plan Strategy
  - Master Sales Aid Overview
  - Clinical Reprint Overview
  - Docs2Us.com Overview
  - Sales Execution
  - Sales Plan Execution
  - Call Plan Execution
  - Meeting Review
  - Company Vision
  - Closing Remarks
- Workshops
  - Master Sales Aid Training
  - Clinical Reprint Training
  - Call Plan Workshop
- Role Play
- Reception/Dinner
- Award Dinner
- Post-Meeting Communication

Each and every one of these elements should have its own Outcome Model™ as the basis of how you develop and execute it. That's right! That's essentially 21 "mini-outcomes" that have to be determined. The people who are responsible for the development and execution of these elements should undertake their own Outcome Model™ processes as they develop their part of the program.

Don't give me that look.
If you want to take your program from good to extraordinary and *squeeze every bit of return out of your investment,* you will do this. Using The Outcome Model™ for individual program elements isn't as

hard, because the scope isn't as broad; however, each element deserves the same kind of discipline and intellectual rigor as the overall program.

I do this with executive speeches all the time. Let's take a quick look at the V.P. of Sales' speech, "Grow Share by 3 Points!" What would The Outcome Model™ tell us what he needs to do?

DESIRED OUTCOME:	100% Attendee "certification" for every relevant competency
CHANGE IN AUDIENCE BEHAVIOR:	Understanding the Call to Action Buying-in to the Core Message Committing to attendance, assignments, engagement for each workshop Completion of every training module Full Engagement in Role Play Completion of competency testing
CORE MESSAGE:	Competency is required for execution
NECESSARY CONTENT:	Core Message How execution equals share gain Required competencies Tools for achievement Call to action
COMMUNICATIONS VEHICLE:	General Session presentation
BUILD PROGRAM BASED ON CONTENT:	Outline

This stuff may look simple. But ask any professional meeting manager how hard it is sometimes to get a group of sales professionals to engage fully in every workshop, and you'll discover that the elements of this simple opening presentation may be absolutely critical to the overall outcome. *In fact, how this speech is presented may be the key to a 3-point-share gain worth many millions of dollars in revenue.*

Kinda makes you want to pay a little more attention to it, huh?

Keeping outside vendors in line.
Everybody uses outside talent to execute. If they didn't, there wouldn't be any outside talent! They are a valuable resource, with scads of cre-

ativity and a lot of great ideas. All you have to do is run herd on them. Because many creative people go through some form or another of The Outcome Model™ intuitively, they're likely to say "yeah, yeah, right, right," when you present your conclusions to them. Don't be fooled. Most of them aren't listening as well as you think they are. The reason they're not listening is because their individual outcome will *always* be different from yours. Why? Because their outcome is focused on *their outcome!* There's nothing wrong with this; it just needs to be managed.

For example, your outside vendor may have seen something work for another client and want to apply a similar approach to your requirements. Not so fast! Only if the vendor is well-versed in the discoveries you've made through the process is he or she capable of suggesting an element or approach. Be wary of solutions that don't come from the process!

Ideally, trusted suppliers should be included in the process from the beginning. This will improve their approach, increase their creative breadth, inform their ideas and ensure *their* loyalty to your outcome as a their measure of success.

The people who execute your project should care more about your outcome than anybody else in the world!

If they do, when you measure your final outcome, you'll be very happy indeed.

CHAPTER NINE

Measuring

the Outcomes

"The only man who behaved sensibly was my tailor;
he took my measurement...every time he saw me, while
all the rest went on with their old measurements
and expected them to fit me."

- George Bernard Shaw

My wife and I sat in the front seat—our friends Craze and Jennifer in the back—as we drove south along the rocky shores of the Atlantic Ocean one summer afternoon several years ago. We had been in Kennebunkport, and had driven up to look at President George H.W. Bush's house. The president came out and waved and then sped away with his grandchildren in his speed boat.

We'd been on our little road trip for three days, and the four of us had pretty much exhausted the conversation along the shores and back roads of Maine, so we settled in for our trip back to our place on Cape Cod. The car was skimming along the road rhythmically, the air conditioning quietly humming. I'd found a sixties station on the radio, and as I drove, my passengers seemed to be nodding off. Then, out of the cool, calming, quiet came Craze's voice, as if from far away.

"Hey, Bruce. I bet I've done something you've never done."

"What's that?" I asked.

"I bet you never closed your head in a car door."

"What?"

"I bet you never closed your head in the door when you were trying to get in your car," he said.

I wasn't exactly chagrinned to admit that I hadn't. He explained, in depth, how he'd done it, how he'd practically knocked himself out, how his son had asked him, "Daddy are you okay?" And how he'd told him, "No I'm not okay... didn't you just see me close my head in the [expletive] car door?"

Craze has done many things I haven't. Here was just one more example. I made the mistake of thinking the story was over.

"It can't be done," he said. "I've tried it since. Several time, in fact. It's physically impossible."

So, now we know.

We simply can't assume results from anecdotal or non-relevant evidence. Just because something worked before, or even because you think it looks like it worked, doesn't mean it did or that it will again. Previous successes may be predictors of future successes; however, they guarantee nothing. That's why we have to keep measuring! Just because you closed your head in a car door once, doesn't mean you will (or even can!) close your head in a car door again.

The Outcome Model™ will do absolutely nothing for you without measurement. If you forget everything you read in this book except the chapters on identifying an outcome and measuring it, you'll be better off than when you started. Measurement of the desired outcome pays your way. It proves your worth. It helps you identify what works and what doesn't. It even gives clues as to why one thing worked while another thing didn't.

I said early on that if you use The Outcome Model,™ you'll achieve your outcome. Measurement is the only thing that will prove that statement.

You have to measure every time. If you repeat a program, a video, or a training module over and over again, you still have to measure it against your desired outcome. Why? The outcome may have changed. The audience may have changed. The entire cultural dialogue may have changed! You won't know unless you measure.

You've heard the old adage, "If it ain't broke, don't fix it." I agree. But how do you know it ain't broke if you don't measure it? The fact is, you don't. You can be rolling right along, spending money, feeling great, communicating with your colleagues or customers, and for all you know they've stopped listening, or even worse, they're talking about you behind your back.

My car is spying on me.
Speaking of talking behind your back, my car calls my dealership service department when something needs to be fixed on it. Yes, that's creepy. I'll get in, turn my radio to 1970's soft rock, and the display will read "Due for Service." Assuming the car isn't remarking on my taste in music, I take it in for service.

This always annoys me, because the car's running great. But it's the only way I would know when need a brake flush. The car manufacturer has

153

built in a measurement tool that supersedes the measuring I would normally do by taking the car in regularly to see if it needs a brake flush. That's because, the average guy like me isn't going to do that!

I'm not going to check it myself, and I'm not going to take it in to have somebody else check it. I'm lazy (or ignorant) that way. The technology is forcing the measurement upon me. But it's not just to annoy me. Measurement of the viability of the brake fluid ensures successful braking when braking is required.

Braking is important. Ask Thelma and Louise.

You may tell me I'm preaching to the choir. If that's the case, why aren't more people measuring consistently and successfully?

There are five basic reasons people don't measure the performance of their program in delivering their desired outcome:
1. They don't think it is measurable
2. They don't know how to measure an outcome
3. They're afraid to measure themselves out of a job
4. Measurement always yields the same results
5. They're not experts in measurement

I haven't really met anybody who feels that measurement is not important. More than ever, in good economic times and bad, the whole notion of return on investment is a central theme associated with almost any expense. The question of what we get for our money is starting to be asked openly and pointedly. So, really, the reasons we've listed for not measuring aren't going to convince the people who are keeping an eye on the money.

THE OUTCOME MODEL™ ETERNAL TRUTH
Everything is measurable.

The measurement of any outcome depends entirely upon how the outcome is chosen and defined. It is fairly safe to say that anything can be measured, as long as it can be quantified against something. All measurement is relative. It's either relative to a number, a timetable, or a quantifiable business result.

You can even measure a general feeling, but you're likely to have a hard time supporting a causal relationship between good feelings and a financial return. People who get free tickets to a ballgame are going to have good feelings; but they don't result in ticket revenue. People with good feelings don't always pony up.

THE OUTCOME MODEL™ ETERNAL TRUTH
How you measure is based on the outcome itself.

Measuring well requires that you really understand what you want. There are all kinds of experts who would argue that I am oversimplifying. But let me be clear. Measurement does not drive *anything.* Measurement is a tool to find out if your strategy and tactics are effective. That's it. It's like counting money in your wallet. How much do you have? How much *did* you have?

The key to The Outcome Model™ is to define an outcome that is measurable. You define the parameters of measurement when you define your outcome. The outcome might be a quantity, level of quality, an amount of time, a favorable or unfavorable impression, or a sale versus a no sale. The more specific the outcome, the more easily measured that outcome will be. You'll also find that the more relevant to actual business outcomes your defined outcome is, the better it will sit with your management team.

Not long ago, a client engaged us to produce a tradeshow exhibit campaign that would help "define their brand as customer-focused." After a great deal of back and forth regarding the ultimate outcome, we created a live theater program offering a series of lifestyle demonstrations on cooking, fitness and nutrition.

From the very beginning, the program was a huge draw, and exit polling showed it as the most memorable activity in the exhibit. Visitors were also asked to define the company's brand, and the results were remarkably positive, with respondents using the phrase "customer-focused" more than we could have dreamed of. Finally, random timings were taken of individual visitors' investment of time in the exhibit showed that people who attended the program stayed inside the exhibit more than 10 times longer than the average exhibit stay. 10 times longer!

However, true success (as measured in ROI) came several shows into the schedule. That's when we defined an outcome that would have a measurable effect on revenue. History showed that sales increased directly proportional to product demonstrations. If you could get a prospect to spend time on the details of the product, you were more likely to sell him or her. We knew we had a winner with this program; our job became transitioning visitors from the program to a product detail station.

We defined our outcome as a desired number of product details per day. With some intensive training for our sales representatives in ways to move the visitors from the program area to the product area, we exceeded these goals. Our measurement showed a marked increase in product demonstrations driven by a program that drew attendees, defined the company brand as customer-focused, and opened them to hearing more. Our measurement proved the program a success.

THE OUTCOME MODEL™ ETERNAL TRUTH
If you measure yourself out of a job, it's because you got a better one.

I have actually heard people say they were afraid to measure, because they thought they might prove what they do to be non-essential. That's certainly a possibility. If you're a director of consumer advertising and measurement proves that advertising to the public has little or no impact on your revenues (and, therefore, costs more than it brings in), chances are your department is on the way out.

On the other hand, if you're the one who proves that there are better ways to spend the company's money, and then can suggest what those ways might be, it's a good bet you're on your way up.

A client at a large corrugated paper company measured himself out of a job and into a better one. He began to take a close look at their trade advertising and trade show exhibits budgets and discovered that the millions of dollars spent were resulting in the same, fairly flat, numbers in production for their relevant clients.

Taking a close look at who bought what from them, he determined that really, when it came to a significant contribution toward their bottom line, only about 200 clients across the WORLD were appropriate targets. And, most of them were customers already!

So, think about it. If you look at the spend-to-return ratio on trade shows and trade advertising for this company, you'll see they were layout out millions of dollars to reach people they didn't really even want to sell to!

So he closed up shop. That's right. He cancelled all trade shows and trade publication advertising, in essence, writing himself out of a job.

But he had a better plan. He developed a proposal to create an "innovation institute," an actual building with product and package designers and engineers, where existing customers and top-notch targets could come, at the corrugated company's expense (money that wasn't being spent on trade shows and advertising!), to talk about ways to increase the effectiveness of their packaging and to increase profits for the customer.

Of course it worked! It was like The Outcome Model™, focusing on the customers' outcomes as a way of adding value to the relationship. The company picked up several new large accounts and increased income from existing accounts by an unheard of amount.

Measuring the return on what the company had "always done" resulted in this brilliant man measuring himself right out of one job and into a much better one! He actually went on to become the head of a major product area within the company later on.

THE OUTCOME MODEL™ ETERNAL TRUTH
Measurement will never yield exactly the same results from project to project.

If you don't think this is true, ask Al Franken and Norm Coleman. They're the senate candidates from Minnesota whose election in 2008 was decided only after eight months of recounts and legal wrangling. If you can't get the same results out of the same numbers, it's a little presumptuous to expect you'd get "the same results" for entirely different programs.

If an outcome is precisely derived, the measurement of that outcome should change with just about every variable. I would go so far as to suggest that if you get the same results from two different samples, you're probably making some mistakes in the model or the measurement.

The most common mistake is an ineffective scoring system, which offers very little differentiation between success and failure. If total success is a "5" and total failure is a "1", what have you learned from a composite score that is a "3"? That there were some successes and failures? Possibly. That everybody thought the offering was average? Maybe. That some people just tend toward the middle? Could be.

If you are measuring your outcome by sales increases or hits on a web site or delivery of product demonstrations, your understanding of the outcome is better, but you must constantly assess the level at which you consider your effort successful. If you achieve your sought-after 2 point market share increase through a sales promotion, shouldn't you continue to increase market share if you offer the same promotion the next year? Or, are the targets of the first promotion different from the targets that would allow you to continue to gain share year after year?

Citius, Altius, Fortius.

Just because the numbers are the same doesn't mean the numbers define success over time. "Citius, Altius, Fortius" is the Olympic motto, which translates "Swifter, Higher, Stronger" and suggests that the same numbers year after year are not, by any means, a measure of success.

This is the danger of the statement, "we've always done it this way, and it always works." If you get 1200 product demonstrations at a trade show every time you do it, can you always assume that 1200 is the right number? Are there more effective ways (like the aforementioned "Innovation Institute") to drive your ultimate outcome? Are product demonstrations even an effective measurement for ultimate success in driving sales? If so, to what extent?

Precision measurement results in a precise understanding of what is going on. Precise measuring should pretty well insure that every result is different from the previous one. But, overall, measuring should encourage us to find ways to improve our outcome every time. If we're not doing that, we're not challenging ourselves.

THE OUTCOME MODEL™ ETERNAL TRUTH
You don't have to be an expert in measurement to measure effectively.

I don't claim to be an expert in measurement! If you are a testing expert or a statistician or a market researcher, you've probably already torn this chapter out of the book yelling, "Philistine!" You've looked at my credentials (such as they are) and you're calling all your friends in the business to tell them that some guy with a background in writing is talking about measurement. You're appalled at my attempt to have anything to say on the subject.

All I can say is, "simmer down." I wouldn't dare put my 1976 stack of key-punch cards up against any of the technologies you guys are using to measure behavior. I admire you. I really do. I don't necessarily want to have dinner with you, but I admire you.

What I admire is that you are interested in finding ways to measure more quickly, more precisely and more deeply. But no matter what you tell me, your technology shouldn't drive what is measured. Your technology should simply measure it.

What I mean is this. Measuring an outcome is and will always be a human experience. It will always be about identifying an outcome that is relevant, realistic, and measurable… and then determining whether you achieved it. It might be done on a super computer, or it might be done by counting tickets. It doesn't matter. However sophisticated it needs to be… it simply needs to be done.

Technology gives us more options that we ever had when it comes to measuring and laying out the data. But the technology will never choose your relevant outcome, and it will never be able to replace the simple human understanding about why humans do what they do, buy what they buy, or interact the way they interact. That's what they pay you for.

THE OUTCOME MODEL™ ETERNAL TRUTH
Measuring is not enough. What you do with results will determine the success of your measurement model.

I recently worked with a client in the financial industry whose customers depended on a wide-ranging market research instrument that the company put together for them annually. In a recent user-conference, a discussion regarding the importance of this initiative revealed that while the customers wanted the data, few, if any of them, had ever read a single page of it.

This is a cautionary tale, not because money was wasted on the study, but because valuable information went unheeded. Important results that might change the way these customers went to market was ignored. They had the data on their credenzas, and it looked really important there… but they didn't do a thing with it.

If The Outcome Model™ is to be effective, it is essential that we change what we do by the results of what we measure. All too often measurement is used either to pat ourselves on the back or point fingers at others. Measurement is intended for neither. It is intended to provide information that will help us fine-tune or change our approach to doing business, so that we can do business *better*.

The Outcome Model™ is never complete until we do something with what we learned.

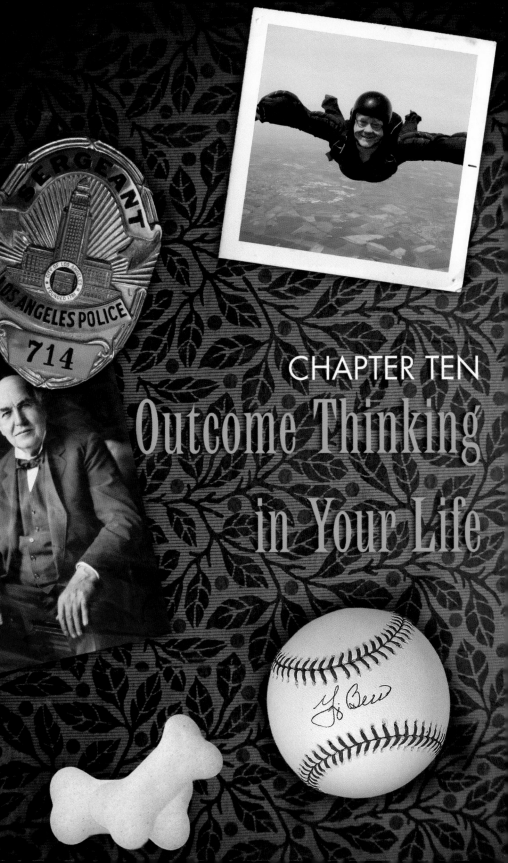

CHAPTER TEN

Outcome Thinking
in Your Life

"God promises a safe landing but not a calm passage."

- Bulgarian Proverb

Just about thirty-five years ago I was bored. So I went to the student center to see what kinds of activities might be posted for students of my ilk, those bored and bereft of cash and prospects. Back then, of course, there was no internet providing unbounded access to the world of opportunity; there was only a bulletin board with those single sheets of paper where you tore off one of the phone numbers at the bottom if you were interested. I'm not sure they still put up signs like this, but here's a sample on the left. They were usually put up by people looking to sell a bike or find a roommate or something. I wasn't looking for a bike or a roommate, though. I was looking for fun. My very first roommate in college proved that roommates were seldom fun, unless you got your chuckles from a guy who ended up sleeping under old newspapers and caught himself on fire at least once a semester. He'd have died, too, if there hadn't reliably been a warm, half-drunk beer on the table next to him for fire extinguishing purposes. It had been a dreary first couple of months of school, and I needed to get out of the dorm and maybe do something I hadn't done before. This wasn't going

LEARN TO SKYDIVE!!!

Free first lesson?
SAFE!
FUN!
WAY OUT THERE!!
NO RISK GUARANTEE!

We'll teach you, then you'll jump!

NO WEENIES, PLEASE

call 555-0348

to be easy for someone who had already witnessed self-immolation at the tender age of 18. I mean, there just aren't that many things that can rival watching somebody burn himself up and put himself out with beer… several times!

Anyway, it didn't take long before I came upon a sign offering "Free Sky Diving Lessons!"[33] Now there was something I could sink my teeth into… and, better yet, get killed doing it to boot! Talk about a magnet for a highly mature college freshman! It was an easy decision, and I tore off a number.

The next morning I met the van, painted with a cartoon "Keep-on-Truckin'" looking dude in a parachute and the phone number 804-423-DROP, out in front of the student center and piled  in with five or six other bleary-eyed students. It was an early call, and we were sucking on Styrofoam cups of bad coffee. The guy next to me was eating a convenience store burrito from the "Lucky 7," which was something I could have done without, and drinking straight from a quart-size carton of chocolate milk.

Next to him, though, was my dream girl.

Her name was Meredith, and she was the off-and-on girlfriend of one of the guys on our hall. A chestnut-haired beauty with almond eyes, she came from the right side of the tracks in Richmond, a prep-school girl with impeccable credentials, meticulously manicured fingernails, and porcelain skin. She told me she was going because she was quite sure

---

[33] It was the old drug-dealer technique: "First one's on me, my man." After that, they figured that anybody who jumped once would be hooked. That's when they started selling them jump suits with their names on them, custom helmets, "parasail" chutes, and all the other accoutrements needed for jumping out of perfectly good airplanes.

skydiving would be "a rush." And she was dressed out for it, too, pearls and all. Together, we settled in (tell me the guy wasn't reaching for a second burrito!) for the long, early-morning drive to Scottsville, Virginia, at the foot of the mountain where "The Waltons" lived on television.

DaVinci's parachute design c. 1483

We found that the jump school doubled as a farm on which the farmer had built a long grass runway by a dirt road and between rows of soybean plants. The school itself consisted of a small out-building that contained, among the skydiving training tools, a variety of indeterminate farm implements used for, I don't know, thrashing things, I suppose.

We learned a lot that morning. How to wear a chute, pack a chute, use a chute; how to jump, spread eagle, turn over, turn back, get oriented; how to deploy the chute, turn, float with and against the wind; how to hit the landing zone, land without breaking anything, roll over, capture your deployed parachute, and gather up your stuff.

We also learned what to do if we were going to land in a tree, how critical it would be to avoid power lines (I knew that one going in), and how to remove the rig from your body if you were going to land in a body of water.

"Don't land in the water," the teacher said, "or you'll die."

Jumping out of a Cessna 182 wasn't at all like the weenie tandem-jumping they're trying to foist off on the public today. Heck, no. Although we were on a static line (which opened the chute for us) we were jumping by ourselves, and it wasn't one of those roomy doors where you merely "step off" like you were getting into a taxi on the way to the clubs on a Saturday night. This was REAL skydiving.

The jump master would give you three commands. They were:
1. Feet out
2. Out on the strut
3. Go!

Here's how it worked. Once the plane was in position so the jumpers would be safely blown back to the landing zone, the jump master opened the door, which slammed loudly up against the wing. When it was your turn, he'd yell "feet out!" At that, you'd hang your feet out of the plane, holding on to the sides of the empty doorway.

Then he'd yell "out on the strut!" You'd put your feet on the tire of the landing gear and reach out for the strut, which is that metal bar that runs from the side of the plane to the wing to stabilize it.

At this point, you're riding on the outside of the airplane, feet on the tire, holding on to the strut, sort of like a wing-walker from those old movies you used to watch on Saturday mornings before your parents got up and the cartoons came on.

The final command was "Go!" When the jump master yelled "Go!" you leaned forward and pushed yourself off, feet behind you in a flying position, arms and legs out to keep you steady. And you dropped like a stone.

The little plane was big enough to hold a pilot, a jump master, and four jumpers if we all held our breath. In fact (and I'm not lying here), as we bounced down the bumpy grass runway and approached the line of tall evergreens at the end, the pilot would yell *"Lean forward!"* and we'd all have to lean toward the front of the airplane so we could get enough lift to make it over the first stand of trees. We never knew if the pilot was kidding or not, but the jump master never laughed, and he was leaning forward, too.

Meredith and I trained side-by-side. They made her take off her jewelry and gave her a big, clunky pair of boots to replace her L.L. Bean duck shoes, but other than that, she completed the course like a pro. Our final test before going up was to jump off a ladder and roll in the dirt, and she took to this like she'd secretly played field hockey or something.

And, as fate would have it, she and I were on the list to go up in the first load. Together, we were to lose our skydiving virginity.

The burrito and chocolate milk guy was looking a little green as we circled the field, but fortunately he was the first to jump, so we were spared what might have "come up" if he'd had to wait any longer. Feet out, out on the strut, and he went. The airplane lurched as he launched himself, and we couldn't see whether his canopy had opened. "Safe," declared the pilot, which we assumed meant the guy was floating rather than plummeting.

Meredith was next. She turned to look at me as she slid along the floor of the aircraft to get in position. And what I saw on that lovely face, in those deep brown eyes... was abject terror. Not the kind of fear you see when you hear a bump in an empty house or the rattling of a locked door at midnight. No, this was the kind of fear you see when the chain saw man has already gotten in and has you cornered in the shower stall. This was the kind of fear that said I guess I'll see you in hell.

"Feet out!" the jump master directed Meredith, and she slid her shapely calves out into the rushing wind.

"Out on the strut!" She reached for the cold aluminum bar and curled her fingers around it in an elegant death grip. And now this beautiful girl was riding high on the outside of the little Cessna, the strands of hair that had escaped from beneath her helmet reflecting the autumn sunlight like optic fibers.

"Go!" The jump master's voice was like a high-powered rifle.

"No!" Meredith yelled back with equal caliber.

"Go! You gotta GO!" the jump master screamed.

"No and NO!" Meredith countered.

So with that, the jump master kicked the girl of my dreams off the strut and into the void of a crisp, autumn, Virginia sky.

Intuition plus understanding.
The real purpose of The Outcome Model™ is to attach a contextual discipline to an intuitive process. This allows us to be creative and thorough at the same time. We know it's the right path. We know we have to have the answers to certain questions before we can dig for answers to other questions. We know we have to know our destination before we can plan how to get there. The Outcome Model™ provides this pathway.

The Outcome Model™ is very intuitive. Many of us practice it daily, certainly on the simple stuff like getting the paper or feeding the dog. It's pretty intuitive to open the can before putting it in the dish, to have the dish in place below the can before we pour it in, to put it on the floor so the dog can reach it. It's hard to screw that up, unless maybe you're a teenager.

I am obsessive-compulsive enough that I have tried to find the shortest distance between the *idea* of feeding the dog and the successful execution of the dog's dinner. This intricate process involves how I carry the bowls, where along the way I put water in the water dish, which elbow I use to turn off the light in the laundry room, etc., etc., etc. Sometimes my wife says, "just let me feed the damn dog." Dinner is more complicated than breakfast. At dinner she gets chicken broth (the dog, not my wife).

Because The Outcome Model™ is intuitive, we may be seduced into thinking that it's a no-brainer. This is a fatal mistake, because every step has to be done correctly in order for subsequent steps to be successful. And, every step has to be done. Because it is a linear process, it requires each step to be completed before the next is undertaken.

The other reason The Outcome Model™ isn't a no-brainer is that it takes lots of brain-power. It takes knowledge, intuition, careful study, research, honest evaluation, and a willingness to change one's mind. It takes openness, honesty, and integrity.

The Outcome Model™ requires more than your brain. It truly requires an investment of your heart and soul.

You have to want to achieve the outcome for you or for another person. You have to look inside yourself to understand the motivations, behaviors, and compelling arguments for achieving it.

You have to believe that it can be achieved, and invest both emotionally and intellectually in its achievement. You have to care whether you succeed or fail. You have to care whether your client or friend or loved one succeeds or fails.

If you've ever watched your young child on stage at a recital or up at bat in a baseball game or trying to piece together an airplane model for the first time, you know what it means to be invested in another person's outcome. You know what it's like if you've watched your younger sister get ready for the prom or your older brother take his driving test.

You know what it's like if you've ever sat in a hospital waiting room while your parent was in surgery.

The Outcome Model™ is about living, breathing outcomes. It's about things that matter. Sometimes, it's even about life or death. For The Outcome Model™ to work, it has to be about commitment and caring.

I would not be the first person ever to write that some of that commitment and caring has gone out of business. I'm sure there's an article buried in every paper in every major city in the world this very day, that has as its subject the declining loyalty of employer to employee, or vice-versa, or the decline of once-great service providers.

According to the Bureau of Labor Statistics, the average person born in the later years of the baby boom held nearly 10 jobs from ages 18 to 36. This included 2.6 jobs at ages 28 to 32 and 2.0 jobs from ages 33-36.[34] That was for people born between 1957 and 1964. I imagine those numbers have gone up for younger people in the work force, although no recent long-term study has been published.

Employees are clearly less committed to their employers than in the past, and employers don't guarantee a lifetime of work anymore. The dynamic of company loyalty has changed.

It's for economists and social scientists to decide whether this is a good or bad thing for our society. I won't attempt any analysis here, because (as in many things) I'm not qualified to figure this stuff out. Somebody important would surely call me on it.

But what I will say is that in a time when some of the traditional ties that bind us to our jobs or companies aren't as tight as they used to be, it is even more important for us to have a *personal commitment* to individual outcomes than ever before. For it may be the things we've achieved rather than the people we've worked for that will define our legacy.

The Outcome Model™ is about how we, *as individuals,* approach our lives and our businesses. If we think this way, if we commit to successful outcomes, if we are willing to do the hard work of achieving these outcomes through careful analysis and logical steps, then we will be successful in whatever our chosen field or job.

---

[34] United States Department of Labor, Bureau of Labor Statistics press release, August 27, 2002, (USDL 02-497).

The Outcome Model™ is a successful approach in any business or culture. It doesn't rely on subjective analysis. With it, your performance is judged on, as Sgt. Friday used to say on the show *Dragnet*, "just the facts, ma'am."

A little bit of love.

I've often thought doing business was a lot like dating. Much of our motivation has to do with pleasing another person, coming up with ways of making her feel special, being creative in the ways we choose to communicate with her.

What takes business from the casual dating realm, which is mostly transactional, to the long-term relationship stage is love. We actually have to care what happens to the person with whom we have the relationship.

I can't work with a customer unless I love him or her… just a little bit.

If this seems creepy to you, let me ease your mind. I mean I have to care about what happens to my customer. I have to care whether he or she is happy in his life, her career, their jobs. I have to understand where their work goals fit into their life goals. I have to understand their business outcomes in the context of their lives.

Granted, I don't always get to know this stuff. People are private, and I'm not going to pry into their personal lives. But if I can gain a broader understanding of who they really are, my work on their business challenges becomes that much easier.

This is because The Outcome Model™ is like any data-handling program. The better the information you feed into it, the better the information you get out. A broader understanding of the people involved in your outcome will result in a more thorough understanding of the steps necessary to achieving the outcome.

Courage and commitment.

The Outcome Model™ will not work without courage. That's because by engaging in it, you have made an up-front commitment to seeing a goal through to its realization.

I don't want to be too hard on modern business here, but a decisive plan for achieving a desired outcome isn't always the hallmark of these cumbersome (and management-heavy) organizations. Like the big old chest-of-drawers in your grandmother's bedroom, they're hard to move around.

It's sometimes hard to achieve a consensus among people with different bosses and different personal agendas. And, in the end, being accountable for a final outcome is a risky business in an organization where anonymity is sometimes the path of least resistance.

This doesn't let all of us self-satisfied entrepreneurs off the hook either. Too often, people in our organizations are afraid to drive an outcome because our companies are so personality-driven that it's expected all goals come from the top. The Outcome Model™ empowers people with brains, knowledge, courage, and the audacity of a good idea to pursue that good idea, whether they're at the top or not.

It takes courage to take the reins, which The Outcome Model™ requires us to do. But with support from management, the proposition is much less scary… and will be much more fruitful.

No titles allowed.

And here's something that does have to come from the top: permission and engagement. Company leadership has to embrace and engage in the process, and they have to participate not as a titled land-owner, but as an equal shareholder. In The Outcome Model™, the discovery of necessary behavior changes and core messaging requires a broad perspective and, in many cases, ongoing personal contact with the people whose behavior you're trying to change. Often as not, senior management doesn't even know these people, let alone work side-by-side with them on a daily basis. We need the people who do if we're going to get a true picture.

That means no titles during the process. Yes, I want to know that she comes from sales, and he comes from product marketing. But I don't want to have to care whether she's a V.P. or he's a Senior Director. It is certainly okay to be the boss. Just not during the outcome process.

What makes business and life fun?

Mystery. Surprises. Discovery. Trying new things. Finding out you can do something you didn't know you could do. Games. All of these things make life fun. And unless you're very different from me, the wall between who we are and what we do is paper-thin. You can't leave your real-life life behind, just because you're spending ten hours a day in a buzzing, fluorescent box of an office or cubicle.

Business is only fun if it, too, involves discovery, growth, new experiences, and maybe even a surprise or two. The Outcome Model™ takes the mundane out of business. It adds spice because it encourages growth. It adds discovery because it's all about discovering things. Discovering things about yourself, your capabilities, your limits, and your horizons. The Outcome Model™ makes business and life bigger.

Discipline is like muscle.

But if you're going to get bigger, you're certainly going to want that new bulk to come from muscle rather than fat. And that takes discipline. The Outcome Model™ is, in itself, a discipline.

If the word "discipline" scares you, believe me, it terrifies entrepreneurs and "free spirits" like me. We're used to doing everything ourselves, in our own way, on our own timetables, and usually out of our own incredibly intelligent brains.

Remember Thomas Edison's statement about invention being 10% inspiration and 90% perspiration? Lots of us entrepreneurs think more like Yogi Berra. We'd say our success is 90% inspiration, and the other half is god-given talent!

Discipline rolls around on our tongues like a lemon rind, sour and bitter. But as it relates to The Outcome Model™, discipline should not be seen as constraint. Discipline is like muscle. It takes a while to train and build up.

There's a method to it, and it's not without some pain.

Ultimately, this kind of discipline, like strong muscle, carries your farther, faster, and with greater ease. It helps you lift more, do more, and achieve more. Discipline, like that inherent in the Outcome Model™, is an engine for the right kind of growth.

The Outcome Model™ should be seen and treated as an important life-discipline. It should be undertaken because it transforms you.

Read the directions before all else fails.
For those of them who have not thrown this book into the fireplace by now, the concept of reading and following directions before proceeding must come as a supreme shock to the system of many modern businessmen and women for whom "Quick Set-Up" is the only part of the user manual they ever see. They mostly subscribe to the "If all else fails, read the directions" methodology, where instructions are mistaken for packing material and cables are color-coded.

The Outcome Model™ is all about reading and following the directions. It's a consecutive process by design. If you don't finish every step, you haven't completed the process. If you don't finish every step in order, the achievement of your outcome is doubtful. If you do achieve your outcome without stepping through the process properly, it's probably an accident. And accidents are no more repeatable than my friend Craze closing his head in the car door. As he said, "I tried it; it can't be done."

Resistance to change.

You may have decided, after reading this far, that The Outcome Model™ is perfect for you or your business. But you may still be reluctant to use it or present it to your managers or peers because it requires people to change the way they work, even the way they think.

Woodrow Wilson said it best: "If you want to make enemies, ask them to change something."

But I encourage you to see The Outcome Model™ not as a change in the way you do business, but rather as a harnessing of the energy and creativity that exist when you or your business are at their best. It is a process that harnesses the power and knowledge that already exists. It's like the clear jar you used to capture lightning bugs when you were a kid; capture enough, and you could read by them.

And while we're on the subject of lightning bugs, there's a wonderful line by Mark Twain, which if massaged slightly, would very aptly describe what The Outcome Model™ does for you when you find exactly the right way to approach the achievement of your outcomes. I'll leave it the way he wrote it, and let you make the creative leap.

> "The difference between the right word and the almost right word," he said, "is the difference between the lightning bug... and lightning."[35]

That's what it feels like when you achieve your outcome. The energy and electricity of deciding exactly what you want, and then taking all the steps to achieve it, is magical.

---

[35] From a letter to George Bainton (1888).

It's lightning that you hope will strike you more than once. And it's attracted only to the people who are willing to do what it takes to commit to an outcome without a doubt that they will achieve it.

The Outcome Model™ isn't about change. It's about transformation.

And now, it's time to GO!
When the jump master kicked Meredith off that little Cessna, she went spinning awkwardly into the cool Virginia sky. The wind was rushing by the open door, so none of us inside could hear what, if anything, she may have said following her upending. It couldn't have been nice. It certainly wasn't something they taught her at that fancy prep school in Richmond.

No more than a couple seconds after her pretty plunge, a billowing chute appeared, and the lovely Meredith made her way back to earth softly, like a puff of dandelion. That had to be both a relief and, as I experienced it, a wonderful ride down. In fact, I always enjoyed the canopy ride more than the free fall simply because free-falling suggested to me, in its very tone, imminent death, an unattractive option at that point in my life.

I like to imagine that once she'd gotten over the shock of being thrown as a mustard seed to the wind, and once her chute had opened without flaw or foul, Meredith might have enjoyed the gentle descent as though she were on her cool, white-columned front porch, sipping lemonade from a sweating tumbler, calmed by the gentle motion of her wicker rocker, the ceiling fan offering a waft of voiceless breeze to keep her tender upper lip dry, unblemished by the slightest bead of perspiration.

Anyway.

The point is, Meredith almost never experienced any of that. She went into *jumpus interruptus*, which was a dangerous choice indeed. The jump master later said that trying to get her back into the plane would have been much more dangerous than kicking her off.

She could have slipped, bumped her head, gotten caught in the strut; her chute could have opened and tangled in the landing gear; she might have become fouled in the static line. Of all the things that could have happened by stopping in the middle of the process... all were bad.

So his exit strategy for Meredith included one leather boot and a properly executed swift kick. He said he regretted it. For a second.

But see, here's the thing. Meredith did everything she needed to do in preparation for her jump. She understood the ramifications, went through the instruction, practiced contingencies, even put on ugly shoes (gasp!). But she wasn't going to commit when the time came to go.

It's the one flaw in The Outcome Model™. The Outcome Model™ is operated by people. And people sometimes won't pull the trigger. When they do, it's great. Things work out. Outcomes are realized. When they don't, well, they either muck up the works or get kicked out. The latter was Meredith's fate.

She never went skydiving again. Oh, and we never dated. Ever. Never went out even once. She wouldn't go out with a boy who was crazy enough to jump out of airplanes.

But I'm very sure she'll tell you now, she loved the ride.

We're in a people business, this life of ours. We are cursed by hesitation, second thoughts, sometimes stubborn refusal to take a risk. The Outcome Model™ can outthink a lot of that stuff. But it can't make a person any more than he or she is willing to be. That's the stuff of personal choice. And every person gets to make it, one way or another.

What's your choice? I assume you started to make it... when you opened up this book.

The Outcome Model™
Eternal Truths

THE OUTCOME MODEL™ ETERNAL TRUTHS
ON THE MODEL ITSELF:

A desired outcome must be relevant, realistic, and measurable.

Outcome thinking requires specific changes in behavior related to achieving the desired outcome.

Outcome thinking requires passion, creativity, experience, and knowledge, all focused in a disciplined way.

The achievement of a desired outcome will depend on the path you take and the choices you make.

The Outcome Model™ requires those who use it to commit to all the steps and accept accountability for the outcome.

THE OUTCOME MODEL™ ETERNAL TRUTHS
ON IDENTIFYING THE DESIRED OUTCOME:

You have to be able to express what you want before you can ever begin to achieve your desired outcome.

The key to identifying an outcome is to make the problem as simple as possible, but not simpler.

Successful outcome thinkers have intuition, honesty, and great listening skills.

THE OUTCOME MODEL™ ETERNAL TRUTHS
ON IDENTIFYING NECESSARY BEHAVIOR CHANGES:

Identifying a desired outcome requires separating outcomes from behaviors.

Outcomes are corporate, while change in behavior always starts with the individual.

The behavior change must be relevant, realistic, and measurable.

THE OUTCOME MODEL™ ETERNAL TRUTHS
ON IDENTIFYING THE CORE MESSAGE:

People who have a broad base of general knowledge are better at applying The Outcome Model™ than those who do not.

Take care of the sense, and the sounds will take care of themselves.

The Core Message is a brief and straightforward way to communicate the connection between actions and outcomes.

The Core Message is a business message, not a promotional message.

Commitment to gaining the knowledge necessary to achieving the desired outcome is prerequisite to the successful application of The Outcome Model™.

The Core Message filters all the "noise" surrounding a direct connection between behavior and outcome.

THE OUTCOME MODEL™ ETERNAL TRUTHS
ON CONTENT:

Content has three jobs: to inform, to motivate, and to manipulate.

Content must be designed around the truth and must never deceive in any way.

A successful motivator speaks to both the corporate and self-interest.

The best way to gain insight is to ask a clear question and listen to the answer.

THE OUTCOME MODEL™ ETERNAL TRUTHS
ON EXECUTION:

Rigor and discipline in each stage of The Outcome Model™ make the subsequent stage easier and more obvious.

Periodic changes in circumstances that do not affect the outcome should not take the focus from the outcome.

Execution begins with the mechanical delivery of the intellectual product of the outcome process.

Execution can do a lot of things, but above all, it had better "sell pop."

Aesthetic content is only worth the investment when it makes the delivery of the content more effective.

Every executable element should be produced using its own minia-ture Outcome Model™.

THE OUTCOME MODEL™ ETERNAL TRUTHS
ON MEASUREMENT:

Everything is measurable.

How you measure is based on the outcome itself.

If you measure yourself out of a job, it's because you got a better one.

Measurement will never yield exactly the same results from project to project.

You don't have to be an expert in measurement to measure effectively.

Measuring is not enough. What you do with results will determine the success of your measurement model.

INDEX

Sugar, A Spoonful of, 140

Trump, Donald, 20

United States Department of Labor
(USDL), 172

University of Florida, 7, 9

University of Georgia, 8

Van Horne, Bill, 34, 115

Vision, 2, 3, 37-40, 47, 52, 58, 61, 78,
102, 144

Wilson, Woodrow, 177

Workshops, 122, 123, 141, 144